# when mountains move

## sandra miller

 **Lovesake**
PUBLISHING

East Bend, North Carolina

*When   Mountains   Move*

First edition 2004
Copyright ©2004 by Sandra Miller

## Lovesake
### PUBLISHING

4324 Mount Bethel Church Road
East Bend, North Carolina 27018
www.sandramillerministries.com
*e-mail:* lovesake@msn.com

ISBN 0-9754553-0-3

Printed in the United States of America

10  9  8  7  6  5  4  3  2  1

book design and production by
Whitline Ink Incorporated
(336) 367-6914  www.whitlineink.com

DEDICATED TO JERRY AND KIP —
*You've made moving mountains worth the effort.*

# PROLOGUE

FOR THE MOST PART, my life has been like a slow-moving train. Not very showy, just putting along toward a destination, occasionally puffing a little steam. Okay, sometimes lots of steam, but life has caused me to work on my steamy personality. In retrospect, I have a few regrets. But don't we all?

For one, I wish I'd been more conscious that I needed an education. But in my case, the quest to learn came later. When I was in school other things took precedence, like sports and boys. Oh, I made good grades, because being in the Beta Club was important to my popularity status. But making the grade and truly learning were two separate entities. I probably wouldn't have attended a local business college after high school had my daddy not sent in the tuition while I was away on our senior trip. Dear ole Dad, he thought I'd make a good secretary.

But I was eighteen. I didn't know what I wanted to do with my life. I just knew I had this mothering instinct, and I needed to cuddle something that would love me without restrictions. I needed to sleep on Sunday mornings without Daddy's growl demanding I rise and get dressed for church. Wasn't I old enough to decide for myself if I wanted to get up and go to church? I sure thought so.

And the smell of those hard-fried eggs he concocted first thing every Sunday morning was pushing me over the edge. I usually managed to swallow a few bites for his sake. At least the smell was enough to arouse me.

I needed freedom from rules ordering me to arrive and leave at the sound of a bell. Rules that graded me on my performance. Rules that gave me ultimatums if I didn't concur. And growls that dictated when

I got up and went to bed, who I went out with, and how long I stayed. My grown-up, unappreciated self needed a change!

So, exactly one year to the day that I flipped the dangling cord on my graduation cap, freedom rang as I stood in front of the fireplace in my parents' living room and said, "I will," to Jerry Miller, the cuddliest creature I knew. Mama was clearly mad. Daddy was purposely indifferent. But I was free at last! It didn't matter that I didn't get married in the church where I was raised and had always pictured I would—I didn't care for the green painted walls, anyway. It didn't bother me that the wedding gown I'd dreamed of still hung on the rack in the department store—it cost two hundred dollars and that's all I had to pull off the whole wedding. Or that the wedding cake turned over in the trunk of a friend's vehicle en route to our house and had to be repaired. Honestly, I shed only a few tears over all of that.

And I'd grown used to the fact that my parents liked very few decisions I made on my own, especially this one, although I was warmed by the fact that my mom volunteered to return the folding chairs to the funeral home after the ceremony. All that mattered was freedom to dance in the sun without being called to supper. Freedom to sleep until noon on Sundays, if I so chose, and frolic at will with my cuddly prince. So with forty dollars and some change, we headed west in our 1968 yellow Firebird with a black vinyl top, mag wheels, and a thick payment book. We didn't let up speed until we reached the Overlook Motel, which was built on the side of a mountain right before you get to Boone, not much more than an hour's drive from home.

That afternoon we enjoyed a laid-back meal at a big farmhouse that some schoolteachers had opened for the summer. We felt special because we were their only customers. The fact that my groom elected to wash the Firebird with our remaining money the next morning instead of having breakfast should have told me something, but I was still reveling in my newfound freedom. With empty stomachs and pockets just as bare, we conveniently arrived on Jerry's parents' doorstep around lunchtime. I felt my face get warm when his dad laughed and commented that we didn't look any different, but the way my new husband's family joked about things my parents would consider "private" was another freedom I enjoyed.

So the day after our wedding, we parked our bank-owned, yellow sports car in the driveway next to our brand-new, bank-owned yellow (yellow was big in the sixties) fifty-six-by-twelve-foot house trailer, in

which power had not yet been connected. But the lack of power did not deter our zeal to commence nesting; we were two birds (dodo birds, that is!) freshly released from the cage of dos and don'ts. We wasted no time. Nine months and nine days later I had two cuddly creatures to nurture: a tall dark-haired handsome one who asked himself daily what he must have been thinking, and a five-pound ten-ounce, slightly premature bald cutie who bore a striking resemblance to him. Yeah, I was free all right. Free to get up numerous times and feed a hungry infant. Free to roll out of bed and report to a job I hated. Free to sweat over how the electric bill was going to get paid. I wonder if all that freedom had anything to do with my parents looking nauseous in the wedding pictures?

Looking back, I'm convinced that omniscient eyes were watching patiently over us as we made mistakes and slowly learned from them. Although I can picture them rolling as he shook his divine head in response to some of our choices. I'm glad longsuffering is one of his characteristics. And thank God for mercy and grace!

I guess if we had the ability to know what each tomorrow would bring, there would be days we would pull the covers over our heads and cower like a dog afraid of thunder. October 3, 1975 would certainly have been one of those days in my lifetime. If Jerry had known what he would be facing after just seven years of marriage, I'm sure our wedding day would have found him cutting a trail in his yellow bird and never looking back. And who could blame him?

Nah, my little choo-choo filled with I-think-I-cans is hardly book worthy. Except for the incidences when Pisgahs have stepped aside and Rushmores have bowed to a power working for me who *is* worthy. The fact that God would demonstrate his awesome power in this often-deemed brassy and over-expressive girl from the sticks seems worth sharing. But doesn't every life have a story if one would but dare to tell it?

Thank God he is a patient conductor. His gentle hand has held the throttle, keeping the poisonous venom of a lurking enemy whose thrust is to steal, kill, and destroy from totally devouring me. Not to mention my own foolishness, which has opened more than a few diabolical doors. Five decades and miles of riding the rails of rocky terrain have taught me a few things: I don't have to sin, but when I do, I should repent quickly before the weeds of its consequences start wrapping around my feet and I bite the dust of hopelessness; I am the righteousness of God in Christ Jesus, no matter how I feel at the moment or what other people think about me; and God has given me an arsenal in Jesus' blood, his name, and his word, but using it is dependent on my knowledge of the scriptures and my faith in its credibility for me individually.

Age has a way of mellowing you to the point where you can savor the view along the way, and that helps when you're waiting for something. Every day won't afford you an autumn's view of a sun-glistening mountain, but that doesn't mean you can't appreciate the leaf by your foot on an ordinary day. For some reason God seems to reserve those kind of observations for those who've been forced to take life at a slower pace. That has been the case for me, anyway. My journey through life has taken me from performing for acceptance to learning to rest in God's unconditional love. From the devastation of quadriplegia to experiencing first-hand a miraculous touch from God.

The purpose of this unraveling of my life is my attempt to glorify my Lord and to bring hope to others who feel betrayed because life has struck them with a bolt of seemingly irrevocable disappointments. As you turn each page, my prayer is that you will hear the music of wheels softly humming a new tune as they grind out the repertoire to "Mountains move…mountains move!"

# 1

## THE PERFORMER

*For I know that in me (that is in my flesh) dwelleth no good thing; for to will is present with me; but how to perform that which is good I find not.*
—ROMANS 7:18

IT WAS 1987, MY THIRTY-eighth year on earth, nineteenth year as Jerry's wife, and second day of my three-day fast. I scanned the view from our kitchen sink window, hands mechanically rinsing the worst from each dish before placing it in its respectful place in the dishwasher. The grass in our backyard stood straight and even like a butch haircut, and the flap, flap of the loose tin on our neighbor's barn added drumbeats to the music of spring winds. But I was more focused on the spiritual than the natural. Hunger had passed and liquids were keeping me from growing faint. I needed to hear from God more than I needed physical sustenance. I refrained from unnecessary activities. No TV. No radio. I cooked for Jerry and Kip, did my household chores, and interacted with people when unavoidable while still maintaining an attitude of prayer and meditation, listening intently for that still, small voice.

It was there, at my kitchen sink, hands emerged in a menial task, that he spoke. Not audibly. Gently. Yet undeniably to my spirit or from my spirit, I'm not sure which. But he spoke, and neither man nor human logic can convince me otherwise. That he spoke to me was no wonder in itself; God speaks to his children every day. But it was the three-word sentence he said that baffled me: "You're a performer."

The past two years of married life had been torturous for Jerry and me. Something had to give before we both broke. I had come back to Jesus after a spin on Satan's falsely glittered carousel. But Jerry didn't view my repentance as real, and the bitterness he harbored was like acid on his soul. He sought revenge with verbal punches and a lifestyle filled with his own secret sins.

Neither of us had set out to walk away from God. We'd experienced miracles and built a singing ministry together. I knew that my sins were wiped away by the blood of Jesus and he had restored what I nearly threw away, but because of past inconsistencies in my walk, Jerry had lost faith in me and, it seemed, faith in Christianity as a whole. When it came to spiritual things, he had always depended on me to be the sail charting his course, the spiritual leader, and I had let him down.

Moving away from God doesn't happen suddenly like choosing a flavor of ice cream. The enemy isn't stupid enough to lay his muck before you full-blown; he worms his way into lives and relationships. By the time his deception has goaded you to the edge of a cliff, one more step doesn't seem like a big deal. If you're fortunate enough to survive the impact of the fall, the climb back up can strengthen your spiritual muscles and make you compassionate enough to reach out to help others. But that's certainly not God's best, and the risk is greater than most of us realize. Surprisingly, it's not the worldly who will judge you; often it's your pew-sharing friends who will opt for the overkill. Exactly what does one have to do to "lose his testimony" as the religious describe people who blow it? I guess some sins merit getting sanctimonious dirt kicked in your face more than others. I've been the kicker and the kickee over the span of my born-again walk, and I have to confess that the pruning from the latter will temper you with grace to deal with the "hideous sins" of others.

So when God the Holy Spirit spoke those three distinct words to me that day, I had to wonder about their relation to the problem at hand. He's such a practical Lord. He didn't speak in Elizabethan dialect or send Gabriel with a message for me to ponder. Nor did he cause bubbles to spell out words in a sink of dishwater. And what he said was the furthest thing from what I would have expected God to say should he choose to speak to me. I know I didn't conjure those words from some crevice in my gray matter, because they took me by surprise. The encounter left me puzzled to say the least, but I wasn't about to discard my message as insignificant; it was too intense. So I listened with spiritual ears and wept into the dishwater while a remote in divine hands rewound my life.

*     *     *

The huge oaks and maples in the yard of my maternal grandparents' farm represented my audience. It was the farm where I'd spent most of my waking hours from infancy to my ripe-old age of five. Located in a rural area about three miles south of the yawning town we call East Bend (because it's in the east bend of the Yadkin River located in the foothills of North Carolina), a kid could only imagine what the glamorous life of the big city was like. But I had all the open space in the world in which to imagine. You couldn't see another house from theirs—only fields, trees, flowers, gardens, and sky. And, of course, the obligatory farm buildings: pump house, woodshed, corncrib, tobacco barn, pack house, and feed barn.

The painted gray plank front porch of Grandpa and Grandma Davis' three-room house was my stage. A small stick served as my microphone. And the multi-colored scrap material with horses and clowns and one crinkled piece of solid crimson (my favorite) that Granny kept stuffed in the wardrobe draped around me, created my costume.

"*Que serà serà. Whatever will be will be. The future's not ours to see. Que serà, serà.*" I'd often sing. But it was that Andy Williams song, "Moon River," that was thundering from my throat toward my tree audience and caught Mama's attention when she came to pick me up after work one summer evening. I didn't let on that I knew Mama was watching me perform. *She's impressed,* I told myself.

"Well sir, are you going to take after Jake?" she hollered, followed by a hearty chuckle. "He couldn't carry a tune in a bucket!" Before I could respond she headed toward the back porch, which led to the kitchen where Granny always was, and I could hear her voice preceding her. "She can't carry a tune in a bucket!"

Laughter bellowed from the two women whose opinions meant more to me than life. I jerked the makeshift evening gown from my body, ran inside, and crammed the material back into the wardrobe. Nothing else was said by them or me regarding my performance. I was insulted, as much as someone my age could be insulted. Lucky for me the trees never complained about my singing. They even clapped when the wind blew. But now I was bent toward proving Mama wrong.

I was probably six or seven before she decided I could stay on key. That was about the time Kitty Wells came out with a gospel song called "How Far Is Heaven" about a little girl whose daddy had died and gone to heaven. Mama got it in her head that I should get up in front of everybody and sing that tear jerker at church.

"You're singing through your nose," she kept telling me when we'd practice. So she drilled me over and over: "*How far is heaven? When can I go to see my daddy? He's there I know. How far is heaven? Let's go tonight. I want my daddy to hold me tight.*"

It was the saddest song I'd ever heard, not at all like "Moon River," which was sad in a good way. I figured out on my own that "que serà serà" meant, "whatever will be will be," although I didn't understand the significance of saying it in a song. But Kitty Wells' song could move people to consider their mortality. And even though a country music singer performed it, the song did talk about heaven and some-body going there. My singing the song seemed to make Mama happy, and God knows I wanted Mama happy. The song gave me the creeps, though. Who wants to sing a song about your daddy, whom you adore, going to heaven when you're just a tot?

But when the appointed time came, I marched up there in front of everybody and sang "How Far Is Heaven" as loud as I could. Mama had given up on me not singing through my nose, but singing really loud and getting all the words right was worthy of several affectionate pats on the head.

Unfortunately, the old church piano, hidden behind the choir like a black hippo grinning with white even teeth, was desperate for a good tuning. I had memorized the pitch from our piano at home, so I wasn't exactly singing in the same pitch the pianist was playing. But all in all, I felt pretty good about my performance. Until we got home and Mama started spewing over what the preacher said in his sermon after I sang, that is.

"Now people," he spat, "I don't believe in bringing sinful country music into the church. The church ain't no place for it." Then he paused and poured himself a glass of cold water from the pitcher sit-ting on the podium, giving the congregation time to let his comment sink in. After a hearty gulp he wiped his mouth with the handkerchief he kept handy in case foam started settling in the corners of his mouth while he was preaching. He was a hard-preaching preacher the best I can recall. That's the way grown-ups described preachers who worked up a lot of foam like that. He'd sure convicted me of more than a few sins. Why, I wouldn't wear pants any shorter than peddle pushers in the summer for the longest time, even though Mama bought me pretty shorts sets. And I said, "I think" after nearly every sentence just to make sure I didn't tell a lie. And God only knows the guilt I carried after Mama and I skipped Sunday night service to watch Elvis from the waist up the first time he was on "The Ed Sullivan Show." But I think Daddy had a hand in that guilt.

It didn't click with me that the preacher was insinuating my song was sinful. (Maybe because my jaws were salivating over that glass of ice water he was enjoying on that sultry Sunday morning). But after hearing Mama's interpretation, I thought, *I'm bound for hell and it's Mama's fault!* My tiny heart was doing flip-flops.

"He wouldn't have known it was country music if he hadn't seen Kitty Wells' picture on the front of the sheet music," she stormed at Daddy, with hands planted on her hips and fire in her brown and gold-speckled eyes. The conversation was unnerving me, so I retreated to the stoop on the side porch where the summer's sun waited to warm my spirit, summoned my dog, Brownie, and relived the pats on my head. The whole ordeal left a bittersweet gnawing in my gut. Who was I supposed to please, Mama or the preacher? I decided I'd rather please Mama. After all, the preacher never brought me any surprises on payday, and she smelled a lot nicer.

But all that died down eventually, and by the time I reached nine, Mama decided to give my singing career another shot, this time in the secular world where there wasn't nearly as much criticism. I'll never forget that fateful day when she brought home the most beautiful dress I'd ever laid my eyes on. It reminded me of the pink cotton candy I got at the fair each year. The chiffon puffed out like tiny pink clouds at my shoulders and the skirt of the dress felt like layers of whipped cream. It cost a whopping twenty-five dollars—a big chunk out of Mama's piecework check. And it was all mine. Not to wear just anywhere, mind you—it was especially for the second-floor Hanes Knitting Mill Christmas party in Winston-Salem where Mama worked. And yours truly was to be the star attraction, performing "Rudolph The Red-Nosed Reindeer." She never came right out and said it, but the implication that I needed to get it right was strong. Maybe it was the dress, but I felt confident I could pull it off.

When the big night finally arrived, everything fell into place. Except Mama—she was as shaky as Jell-O before it sets up good. You'd have thought that band of T-shirt makers was a jury about to reach a verdict as to the fate of the rest of her life. The only thing making me quiver was the chill on my bare arms in December and my bird legs being exposed to the cold air circulating under all those crinolines. And, of course, the occasional thought of pleasing Mama. But if not arrayed in that garb of pink chiffon, I shutter to think what the outcome of my performance would have been. I looked the part down to my white nylon socks and shiny black patent leathers. Mama rolled my corn-colored hair around her finger until it lay against my neck like a string of perfectly lined sixes. And if there was a smidgen of doubt that I could pull it off, it flew out the window after I entered the big building where Mama worked and got all the compliments about how pretty I looked. I was oblivious to the fact that adults say those kinds of things while thinking, *What an ugly kid.* But I got through my performance without a catastrophe. Santa came with gifts for the kids. My head got patted. And Mama could breath normally again.

It wasn't until a few years later that I found that fulfilling these demands often placed on kids was a challenge I couldn't seem to meet. When puberty kicked in high gear, the cuteness faded away, and I think Mama would affirm that most of the sweetness left with it. I no longer wanted to be dressed up and stood in front of a bunch of people to sing some goofy song. And my body was now playing tricks on me. I realized that growing pains didn't mean your bones were stretching the skin.

For me, it meant having to deal with a menagerie of emotions I'd never experienced as my body bloomed adult-like surprises. Growing up in the fifties and sixties didn't afford kids the openness to discuss what these changes meant, and very few parents, it seemed, were comfortable enough with their own sexuality to discuss such issues with their kids. Why, I don't remember hearing Mama say the word "pregnant" until I was grown. She told me she was "expecting" when I was sixteen. Talk about a thunderbolt!

I also found that there were people now I'd rather please than Mama. People my age, and older, whose opinions meant life or death to my popularity status. Fitting in is everything at twelve, and not to appear "mature" was like being grown up and still having your baby teeth. There was a part of me that was sure I'd reached nubility, with my training bra and all. But another part deep within yearned for the soothing smell of Mama's "Bluegrass" cologne and the brush of her lips on my cheek like a tender smack from a raspberry sucker. I can't pinpoint exactly when she stopped kissing me, probably when I stopped kissing her, but I lost something special when it ended.

Mama wanted me to stay a little girl, but my body wouldn't let me. She wanted me to do everything right and stay on (her interpretation of) the straight and narrow. But I was a wild colt with more energy than sense, and I was sure she could never understand my need not to be treated like a child. So we became like ostriches to the problem. I did a good job of suppressing those lingering little-girl tendencies, but I wish I'd remained undaunted by the pressure to act older than I was. But shoot, back then if you didn't have your husband-to-be picked out by the time you were sixteen, there was a good chance you'd be left behind. I didn't know that I had plenty of time, and if you lived an average lifespan, being an adult would last a whole lot longer than childhood. But woe to anyone who tries convincing an adolescent of that. Hey, my legs needed shaving. And my lashes were screaming for mascara, the thick black kind. And my white lipstick made me look…well, come to think of it, it made me look ridiculous. But it fit the early sixties groove. I did the Twist, the Swim, the Mashed Potato, and teased the fire out of my hair. I'm convinced the sixties are responsible for my temptation to try Rogaine today.

As for Mama, she turned into a drill sergeant. She's been called a banty rooster before, and I can nod to that assessment, not that that's always a bad trait, mind you. But my affectionate pats from admirers were replaced by whops from her if I didn't practice the piano. She made me peck out the alto note with one finger and sing "Heaven Will Surely Be Worth It All" until I came to seriously doubt it ever could be. In my spare time, when I wasn't shooting my basketball through a substitute goal in the fork of an oak tree in our front yard, songs like "Run Around Sue," "The Lion Sleeps Tonight," "I'll Do My Crying in the Rain," and "This Is Dedicated to the One I Love," were spinning on my portable record player. My sand-colored ponytail was now held together by a rubber band and placed in a drawer to remind Mama of the child she could not keep. I wore my cardigans backward, hip-stitched skirts, and of course Weejuns—everyone who was anyone wore Weejuns.

Understanding Mama's persistence when it came to playing and singing church music was usually draining. I felt inadequate, like she was comparing me with every mother-daughter duet, or child pianist that passed through. Why couldn't she be satisfied with the fact that I'd rather shoot baskets than practice piano? It seemed to me that singing for the Lord ought to be spontaneous. I did not comprehend that spontaneity was contingent upon skill. But Mama knew. Her motivating techniques might have been questionable, but she knew, if given the choice, I'd jump ship.

Fortunately, Helen Church came to our Baptist church to hold a singing school just in the nick of time and rescued me from the jaws of Mama's passion. Mrs. Church was as strong-willed as buttermilk and just as adamant when it came to her teaching techniques, but she made learning to sing by notes and playing gospel music a pleasant adventure. Mama immediately enrolled me as one of her students, and the passion became my own. Mrs. Church handpicked an all-girl quartet from our church choir and assigned me the tenor part. We performed all songs in the key in which they were written, and sometimes I thought the veins in my neck would surely burst as I strained to reach an E or an occasional F. But Mrs. Church declared it would not hurt me. Those were good years. We traveled around the area to church homecomings, revivals, and community functions in our navy wool shirts and light blue blouses. It was there that I got the basics for what would eventually work to keep me sane.

And now, standing at my kitchen sink some thirty years later, the inbred yearning to perform was being questioned by my own conscious. Whom was I really performing for? Were my motives pure?

Did God really call me to sing? Should I give it up?

I knew the three words from heaven—*you're a performer*—were the key to unlocking real success in my life. I was a performer from day one, trying to earn everyone's approval, not always making choices from a pure heart. Performing for approval was a self-centered endeavor, which could never produce the right kind of fruit. The God of the universe wanted me to know that keeping his commandments was all he required. He wanted to be my music and song. And he loved me just as I was. He looked past the frills and pink chiffon, and saw my heart. He wanted me to understand that angels applaud at the acts I perform from my heart when no one else is watching. There are no charts in heaven requiring prestige or perfection, just books recording works that will be judged one day by God's standards. And the times that I've blundered and felt like a failure, he continued to recognize me as his child, perfected in his Son. His word reminds me that when real promotion comes, it's neither from the east nor the west. Real promotion comes from God, and no man can demote you when you're walking in the Spirit. Oh, to man's standards it might look like you're being demoted, but God sees the whole picture. The clincher is recognizing that God's way up is sometimes down, and time spent at his boot camp, though often painful, produces the real heroes.

It's taken me years of rising and falling to get to the place where I could have ears to hear the voice of the Spirit. I still struggle with the performance thing, and it hurts when you're rejected. But I have access to a Teacher with unlimited wisdom. He teaches me through the correction of his word, through the godly counsel of others, and through the inner witness of his Spirit. And the lessons have been priceless. When disappointments come we must realize that our lives consist of more than the speck of earth we physically inhabit. "It's not what people do to us that's important, it's how we react to it," I heard a preacher say. I have to remind myself often of Colossians 3:23: *And whatsoever ye do, do it heartily, as to the Lord, and not unto men.* I don't have to be high in the world's standards to be successful, nor do I have to be low to be humble. I don't have to stand before a multitude to minister the love of Jesus, nor do I have to deny myself that opportunity when it comes to prove I'm genuine. Life is not nearly as complicated as we make it.

I'm thankful for a mom who wanted me to excel. Both my parents worked hard to provide for my brother and myself. I had numerous "pink chiffons" because of them. And I'm blessed to know a Savior who would consider me worthy of conversation. A heavenly father who reaches his long arm to earth and gives me love pats of approval when I need them. He is not unreachable. When I don't understand the turmoil, he's waiting to walk me through. When I question his faithfulness, he remains unchanged. When his word seems to contradict his actions, the fact that it is forever settled comforts me. When I'm uneasy with life, his peace saturates me with his own words, written for that very purpose. I know now that I can turn the performer in me loose and be blessed, or I can have a private celebration with just Jesus and me and be overwhelmed with his unconditional love.

And I don't even have to dress for the occasion.

# 2

## STOLEN GOODS

*The thief cometh not, but for to steal, and to kill, and to destroy: I am come that they might have life, and that they might have it more abundantly.* —JOHN 10:10

BELL-BOTTOMS, miniskirts, and polyester leisure suits heralded in the seventies. Afros and long hair parted in the middle were the 'dos. Illegal drugs and a war nobody understood were the demons of that decade. The clean hands of a small, rural town kept my circle of family and friends innocent of many of the culprits of that restless era. Drugs, other than the drugstore kind, were never a temptation to me; I didn't even know where you found them. "Make love not war" was the popular slogan, but free love as exemplified by the hippies was taboo for my upbringing. The seemingly senseless war touched all, though. The peace sign meant very little to the parents, spouses, and children of those on the front lines in Vietnam. And the Civil Rights movement sandwiched many of us baby boomers between an inherited mindset that some things were because they always had been and the fact that mankind would never collectively shift gears, even when right and wrong were as clear-cut as black and white.

I remember Mama telling about helping a neighbor in tobacco when she was a kid, and how it always made her feel sad when they stopped for lunch and everyone ate in the kitchen except a black man in the neighborhood. He carried his food to the back porch and ate alone. Sadly, things changed little until the rise (and fall) of Dr. Martin

Luther King and the war for equality began. If a black family walked into an average all-white place of worship back then, they would not have found a welcome mat at the front door, and, unfortunately, still wouldn't in some churches. Today, some thirty years later, Jerry and I like to visit a predominately black church in Winston-Salem. Bishop J.C. Hash is one of the most anointed teachers of faith and righteousness I've ever heard. Sometimes when I'm comforted by the embrace of the dark-skinned arms of a sister or brother in the faith, and our colorless tears blend in mutual love and adoration for each other and a God who doesn't see color, I feel the urge to fall prostrate before the loving congregation at St. Peter's World Outreach and apologize for the ignorance of my ancestors and my own tolerance of segregation. There are good and bad people in every race, and we should be judged by our actions, not our color. It shouldn't have taken protests and killings to prove that all men are created equal, and yet the Church has been in the Dark Ages for centuries when it comes to equality. Worshiping with saints of color has convinced me that God must have created the black race to keep boredom out of worship services—King David's dance would fit right in at St. Peter's.

In the summer of 1970 I didn't know about the kind of worship that liberates you. I didn't understand that God needs the ministry of our worship, that we were created for that very purpose. I just knew something was missing in my personal relationship with Christ, and that realization was a turning point for me. I had considered myself a Christian since childhood, but I did not know Jesus as Lord of my life; I knew him only as Savior of my eternal soul, my escape route from hell. But now, broken and confused from blotched job attempts and a marriage that left much to be desired, I was seeking him as provider, counselor, and friend. I had bombed out doing things my way; I needed supernatural help. In our day, we thought love was supposed to conquer all, but when you're drowning in a sea of collapsing dreams and your marriage relationship is based on fantasies rather than respect, "love" is not enough. Immaturity played a role in my plummet, but the one thing I felt I did right was also the mortar holding our home together, and he discovered the world on Sunday morning, March 9, 1969, at 9:39 a.m.—nine months and nine days into our marriage.

Kipley Dale forced himself from my body five weeks early, and his smile carved a notch out of my heart that he still holds today. How can a mother caress such a gift in her arms and not be drawn into a deeper relationship with the creator? When I took my first look at his tiny features, all perfectly intact, I knew I was only the vehicle God used to bring such a wonder to earth. I didn't know the specifics then, but I knew there would be days when I'd need access to a higher power. A power that could take over when his little face burned with fever and his chest rattled with every breath. When his bottom lip quivered and tears welled up in his big blue eyes, because he just wanted to stay home instead of going to the babysitter's. I knew he'd need angels to guard him, like when the nurse pushing his gurney toward the huge double doors leading to the operating room turned to Jerry and me and said, "This is as far as you can go." Surgery to repair a hernia might not seem like such a big deal—unless you're just three. And the list of things that tie a parent's hands goes on.

At nineteen and ill-feathered, I was forced to learn to fly in an unscrupulous world for the sake of another whose well-being depended upon my ability to keep afloat. I believe God sent Kip to us early in our marriage as a diversion from our self-centeredness. Neither Jerry nor I always made noble choices—we still wanted to fly with the wind from time to time—but the third person of the Godhead, the Holy Spirit, deity come to earth, had found a place inside me. There was much I had yet to learn about his existence in my life, about the filling of the Spirit, but he was there drawing me to Jesus, even when I pushed him back. How sorry I am for the times I ignored his gentle nudges. How thankful I am for his longsuffering!

It was during my lowest point spiritually that I realized I needed divine help to properly nurture another. That is when I began to question my salvation. It seemed I had more or less evolved into Christianity. I'd been in church my whole life, went through the motions, and had even been baptized. I believed in God and Jesus. But there's a difference in "believing" and Christ dwelling in you. I remember my prayer as if it were yesterday: "Lord, if I'm not saved, save me now. And please lead me to a job that's right for me—I promise to stay there until you say leave."

When Sunday came, I made my profession public when the invitation was given. No one knew it, but a mountain collapsed and fell from my shoulders. A God's kind of love for people swelled inside me, even the ones who didn't return the response. I wept all the bitterness, strife, and confusion away that morning. I started trusting God with the little things, and he became my Lord Monday through Saturday, as well as Sunday. When a friend in the unemployment line asked me to go with her to put in an application at the Western Electric Company in Winston-Salem, I agreed, and the favor of God was waiting for me. I was hired within days as a keypunch operator, and the job was perfect for me. I could program my fingers to do the work while my thoughts wrote a song or pictured Kip as he looked that morning. Sometimes during morning break when I'd eat my peanut butter and crackers that I packed, I'd worry that Jerry might not have enough money to buy himself a snack. I'll never forget the looks from some of my co-workers the day I opened a can of sardines. And I'll never forget what one girl said she'd just as soon eat on a cracker! Many at work thought I was a redneck because I lived in the country, liked Elvis, and carried a Bible in my purse. On my first day at work a girl asked me if I had flown into the city on a helicopter. I laughed, thinking she was surely joking, but her blank stare told me there were actually people working there who were dumber than this country hick.

The odd shift from 10:30 a.m. to 7:30 p.m. worked well for me, especially after Kip started kindergarten. I could fix his breakfast and get him ready to catch the bus, and missing the rush-hour traffic was a blessing in itself. My thirty-minute commute each morning was my time with the Lord, my (yellow) Toyota a sanctuary on wheels. Many mornings I would sail into the huge parking lot at Western Electric like a plane about to land, stunned that I was so lost in prayer that I

couldn't remember crossing the Yadkin River. That time frame of thirty minutes was my fueling for what faced me that day.

Getting home around 8:00 p.m. didn't afford us a lot of quality family time. Jerry's natural love for the outdoors offered him plenty to do. In the summer, he fished. In the fall and early winter, he hunted deer. In the cold months, he ran his dogs in the hunt for quail

*A cowboy Christmas in 1974.* and trapped for fox hides.

His absence took getting used to, but I was just thankful he'd stopped hanging out at the pool hall, which to me was the unpardonable sin. As soon as Kip was old enough (maybe before), Jerry included him in his sports. Hunting and fishing came natural to Kip, also. I'm pretty sure there's a "hunting" gene that has yet to be scientifically named.

I gave up on Kip learning to play the piano after he sauntered across the stage at one of his recitals, pulled a folded sheet of music out of his back pocket and tried (in vain) to get the paper to stay put. The crowd, who knew him all too well, was enjoying his antics, so he continued to amuse them by laying the music down on the bench beside him and playing "Piccolo Pete" by heart in what must have been quadruple time. The fact that he could never remember to bring his music lessons home so he could practice was another hint that my cravings would never be his, so I let it go.

The nearly five years that I worked at Western Electric helped get us on our feet. Jerry had found his niche as an electrician at a local textile plant. He received on-the-job training from a top-notch electrician while going to classes at night to get his necessary certificates. We had both looked forward to 1975, and for the first time, freedom from debt. Finally, there was extra money for new clothes and recreation. A miscarriage the day after Kip's fourth birthday left us both with a hunger for another child. The pregnancy was a surprise, and we hadn't given much thought to the idea of extending our family, at least not until we were out of our bulging trailer. But just knowing that we'd never hold this baby who had been forming inside me for three months left both Jerry and myself feeling empty. The night before I lost the baby, I dreamed that a little blonde-headed boy, in one of those walkers we used to put babies in, was trying to get to our bed, but he could only maneuver as far as the door leading to our bedroom. As badly as I wanted him to come to me, he could not. I look forward to seeing him (or her) in heaven one day.

Something in the spring winds must have aroused Jerry to return to his roots in the summer of '75. I thought he was crazy when he told me he wanted to rent some nearby land to raise a crop of tobacco. I didn't see how either of us could fit anything else into our schedules, but he was set on the idea. I have to admit, in spite of the extra expenses, aggravation to my allergies, and downright fatigue, watching Jerry on a tractor resurrected feelings of ten years back and the first summer we dated. He hadn't had his license long when he lost them for six weeks after a bump up, so I got to keep the Bomb—his '56 black Chevy. Along with the gearstick he had installed was a conspicuous hole in the floor on the passenger's side, which produced a year-round draft and visibility to the highway as you sped along. My head was barely detectable above the oversized steering wheel, but at sixteen did I think I was the stuff!

I tend to attach sentimentally to things I can relate to "good times." Maybe it's the timing, but I've felt a bonding through the years to that piece of land we leased to raise our crop in '75. In the secret place of my heart, I've visualized living in a house on that property. I let my thoughts take me back there from time to time.

*I can see Jerry, his lean back tanned by the summer's sun, tilting to contemplate the neat rows Grandpa Davis' Cub tractor is designing in the red Carolina soil.* I still detect sparks of youthful adventure behind those blue eyes from time to time. I hope they never fade.

*And I see me: frayed cut-off jeans, pink and green plaid shirt, short sandy hair blowing in the warm breeze. My bare feet are spread, firmly planted in the grassy spot at the far end of the field. A black leather holster is draped around my hips, and I'm firing a pistol toward a target Jerry set up near some trees. I'm small, but tough—a modern-day Annie Oakley. On another day my coral bikini reveals places I now try to conceal. I figure I might as well kill two birds with one stone—hoe the field and get a tan. Six-year-old Kip is playing between the rows of tender green plants, which we're hopeful will eventually produce some green in our pockets. Sweat's dripping from skin I should have known better than invite the sun demon to fry, and my right thumb sports a huge blister. Out of nowhere, a glistening six-foot black snake slithers toward us to introduce himself. A scream escapes my lips. I drop the hoe and chant, "Come on Kip, come on," while leaping toward the car like a frightened gazelle.*

I guess my attachment to places and things I once interacted with helps preserve memories of life when things were simpler. Places where the cool brush of a summer breeze splashed relief to my hot cheeks and the moist grass kissed my bare feet. Places where the smell of tobacco curing awakened memories of the boy in the man I love. A time when pain was a mere fleeting interruption of youthful tasks and fatigue a natural experience I could recover from quickly. When open spaces where land and sky touched in photographic splendor freed me to explore without fear or restrictions. A time and a place where I was confident that I was indestructible.

*    *    *

There was a nip in the air on the morning of October 3, 1975. Summer's warmth was yielding to the change of the seasons and the vigil of another kaleidoscopic autumn. A Friday off from school for a teacher's workday and a vacation day from the plant meant a long weekend for Kip and Jerry. They left early, heading to a local diner for breakfast, then to Jerry's uncle's tobacco field to help fill a barn to cure. The first frost was not far away. Our crop was in the pack house, a phase of the process in which my dust allergies forbade my participation—not that I minded. When I think about all that tobacco farmers used to do before taking a crop to market compared to today, it makes me wonder what we're presently doing that is unnecessarily breaking our backs.

Kip leaving early with his daddy provided me an opportunity to sleep a little longer. I pulled my favorite brown wool blanket tightly around my neck in an effort to ward off the chill, but my mind bombarded me with thoughts too serious to allow me to re-enter the sleep mode. It was after 8:00 a.m. before I forced my eyes to open and my toes to touch the cold linoleum. I needed to be out the door and on my way by 9:45 to make it to work on time, but as usual, I left no room for interruptions.

The previous night preyed heavily on my mind. I loved Jerry and felt that deep inside he still loved me, but the flavor was fading from our marital gum. That tingly feeling that young love knows was being snuffed by schedules and deadlines—the real world. We were spending less and less time together, and it seemed as though it had rained on the last flickering spark that once caused a rush of heat. Communication was as stale as last week's toast, which should have been our first warning sign, and life as adults was rudely invading youthful idealism. I was famished from the failure of the previous night's effort to recapture something I'd hoped we'd never lose.

I had planned the night with hopeful vigor, even retrieved a baby blue negligee from the antique dresser crowding our bedroom. My brother had given it to me the previous Christmas, and I was saving it for a special occasion. This was it. My hands pressed the silky floor-length material against my body as I examined every angle in the narrow mirror that stretched from the ceiling to the floor beside the bathroom door. My favorite color seemed to enhance the sadness rather than the hue of my eyes. I sucked in a gulp of air, exhaled, then made my way down the paneled hall leading to the living room where my competitor stood square-faced in a corner giving my husband the diversion of a "Bonanza" rerun.

Jerry was sipping a Pepsi out of a glass bottle and his left arm, resting on the back of the couch, seemed to draw me into it. The eyes that had ignored me for weeks were mortared to the tube. *It's a cover up; he'll melt,* I told myself, and then positioned my shoulder under his armpit. But Jerry could be hard as nails when he wanted to. He was set on ignoring me, but I wouldn't give in easily. I took hold of his dangling hand and forced his arm to fall around my shoulders. Still nothing. So I pretended to watch the western for a while. Patience has not been one of my virtues, especially in my younger years, and mine ran out after the first commercial. I sat straight up on the end of the couch, and if eyes blazing with anger could catch someone on fire, Jerry would have disintegrated.

"You're going to cause me to do something I really don't want to do!" I threatened. His lack of response threw kindling on my anger. I didn't know that I was prophesying my own destiny. I had grown up thinking that if someone didn't treat you right, you had no choice but to retaliate with some kind of action that would put the ball on your end of the court, so to speak. I'm a confronter—a word-throwing, get-it-out-in-the-open, hot-headed debater. Jerry is a passivist—an eye-rolling, wordless, walk-away Joe, which can be lethal to a debater. But we were playing silly games, just like when we were first attracted to each other as high school kids. The only weapon I knew to use was manipulation. The old performer spirit was resurrecting, and not to come out on top was like getting a bad review.

A restless night had surrendered to a new day, but the bitter taste of defeat lingered. I felt frustrated that I could not empty my reservoir of bottled-up feelings; hurt that Jerry didn't need a resolution as badly as I; empty from anticipated reconciliation gone bad; and insecure, because I had drifted from my first love—Jesus.

I pondered my alternatives as I picked the curls out that I'd made two nights before by rolling small strands of fine-textured hair around a pencil and bobby pinning them to my head. It was an Afro attempt that looked more like a dark-blonde Shirley Temple impersonation. The air was brisk, so I searched the closet for something warm. I pored myself into a black acrylic ski sweater peppered with white snowflakes, slid on black dress pants and black ballerina flats. And a black Friday it turned out to be. I can still hear the haunting sound of our trailer door slamming behind me. My Corolla had died sometime during the night. Every attempt at cranking it was futile. I didn't have time for this! Clearly, I would not slide into my workspace by 10:30. But after nearly five years on the job, I'd learned that a "little Coca-Cola" in the bottle smuggled by the guard was an adequate peace offering as long as you didn't make a habit of coming in late. We called the supervisor "Phil," and Phyllis Church could be as hard-nosed as any man if you rubbed her wrong. She was a Pentecostal without the bun, an altogether different version from the "holy rollers" we Baptists heard about, although I don't recall ever seeing her in a pair of pants. And she liked to hire her Pentecostal friends and kids she knew who needed summer jobs. The keypunch department was a medley of Christians and neutrals, teens and adults, dopers and those who'd never even smelled the stuff, like me. I felt Phil would be lenient, because my car not starting was certainly out of my control. I might even get lucky and she would be away from her desk in the corner of the long, rectangular room humming with fingers popping keys and the few remaining older machines spitting out cards like a casino.

The grass sprinkled dew on the top of my feet as I scurried next door to my parents' house. Mark—my only sibling, the surprise that stunned the neighborhood, flabbergasted my grandpa, and thrilled me beyond measure ten years back—sat in a pile of sand between the two lawns creating a demolition derby with toy cars. "Hey, Mark," I greeted him as I jogged by. Mark gave me a glance, but was too enthralled in fantasy to make conversation. Just minutes before, Daddy had collapsed into bed after pulling third shift at the RJR Archer plant in Winston, where he had worked ever since I could remember. I hoped he wasn't asleep yet; the last thing I needed was to irritate him.

"Daddy?" I whispered, peeking into the bedroom that once was mine. A nose emerged from under the powder blue comforter I'd chosen when we moved into that house when I was fourteen.

"What?" he answered with a froggy voice.

*Good, he's not asleep*, I said to myself. "My car won't crank, can I borrow yours?"

A hairy leg surfaced, and I looked away as he retrieved his keys from the pants lying neatly across the chair that belonged to the desk where I used to do my homework. Daddy approached me holding the keys to his Ford LTD and his pants in front of him in an attempt to conceal his red and black polka-dotted boxers. "You'll have to stop and get some gas," he mumbled.

"Great, I'm late already!" I inserted, grabbing the keys. I mumbled, "Thank you," as I sped down the hall.

"High-test," he reminded me.

Mark had moved his pretend Daytona 500 to the sidewalk. "You'd better go on out to Grandma's, hadn't you, Mark?" I asked as I whisked by. Mama was in Nashville, Tennessee, attending a convention for Keller Cosmetics, the company she'd worked for since quitting the knitting mill when Mark was born. It was just like Daddy to assume that Mark had walked through the woods to Grandma Davis' house because he'd asked him to, and just like Mark to put it off until he got ready. It may not have been true in the large cities, but where we live, twenty-five years ago children were considered safe playing in their yards unattended. I got the same response from Mark I seemed to be getting from everybody else those days, but I didn't have time to deal with it. I waved goodbye and backed the long-nosed cocoa-colored LTD out the driveway. My mind was muddled enough with the turmoil on the home front and the fact that I was going to be late, but now I had a dead battery to deal with when I got home. In spite of the brain overload from the night before, two words feathered through my chain of thoughts: Be careful.

Daddy's LTD seemed big and awkward compared to my Corolla, and I wasn't used to an automatic with power steering and brakes. I searched the radio for a country station, hoping to find salve for my bleeding heart. Only weeks before prayer would have been my solution and my radio preference "The Gospel Hour" with Oliver B. Green. Something was pulling me in another direction these days, and I was dismissing that still, small voice. Gas and a little Coke were the present protocol. I stopped at two country stores, but neither proprietor had decided to open—the pros and cons of country living. *Maybe I can make it to Lewisville,* I told myself. Crossing the Yadkin River meant entering Forsyth County and gas stations with normal working hours.

As I breezed down a straight stretch of Old Highway 421 toward the bridge, I glanced down to see where I was on the radio dial. It was only a glance, a mere shift of the eyes, but that's all it took for the brown monster to meander over the yellow line onto the left side of the road. I would probably have been fine if the hood of an approaching car wasn't about to eat mine. The driver let me do the swerving; I was on his side. Instinctively, I jerked the steering wheel to the right. I missed the car, but ran off the right side of the road. Gravel popped like corn under the tires as they squalled in defiance to my driving skills. I wasn't traveling fast, certainly not what one would consider a break-neck speed. My foot was off the gas pedal, and something, maybe a warning from my driver's education days, kept me from applying the brakes. With nails clenched into the steering wheel, I managed to muscle the car back onto the road.

While my little brother was home crashing cars in the dirt, I was experiencing the real thing. And believe me, the challenge was no fun. Somewhere in the midst of the struggle, I realized control was out of my hands. The ride from then on was like hanging upside down on a rollercoaster that had derailed. Gravity seemingly pulled me in the opposite direction from where I was supposed to be going. I was no longer the officer in command of a borrowed ship. The shrill of pine limbs colliding with metal as the car pell-melled over a gully, blazing a trail through uninhabited Yadkin timberland, and a Niagara of glass raining finely upon the rubble is forever plastered in my ears. A towering pine amid a forest of green ended the excursion with an unforgettable thud.

Time may heal wounds, but it bears no ointment for that sound. Every cop's show, every "Dukes of Hazard" rerun, every time I position myself under the wheel of a car, a death bell tolls inside me with the haunting reminder of that event. It is only by the grace of God that I can even ride in a car today. And it is by faith in his word that says he will never leave or forsake me that helps me press through the waves of fear.

Nothing but static from the radio, still in between stations, and the drumming of my heart could be heard after the impact. But the fiasco lingered in my ears like a ghostly echo. I wondered how I had ended up with my face planted in the carpet on the passenger's side—I was not aware of falling. My forehead stung from the broken glass my head had landed in, and a small pool of blood was forming under my right eye. And then it hit me: I had wrecked Daddy's car.

*Well, get up and face the music,* I told myself. I could already visualize Daddy whipping me with words. But when I tried to move, my body rejected my brain like oil rejects water. It was like being buried alive from the neck down. No feeling. No pain. My brain kept giving orders, but my body from the neck down seemed deaf. I was full of life just seconds before, had been since birth. But suddenly, without the courtesy of warning, I was two-thirds dead. And I had to wonder: *Will I soon be dead all over?*

Maybe I did get a warning, but refused to listen. But now I was listening. Now I could pray, wanted to pray. I'd thought I couldn't, that God wouldn't hear with all the stuff that was going on. And really, there was only one prayer at that point I could pray. So I prayed it. Softly. Sincerely. From my heart: *Forgive me.*

That's all I said, and it seemed to be enough, for his response was immediate. There was no demand for justice or penance; it had already been paid. There was no snub-nosed rejection. Not an "I'll think about it" or "I can forgive, but I can't forget" like we humans do. No "I told you so" either. A slipper knows when she's slipping. And he didn't give me a trial run to see if I would be forever true; our spiritual falls come as no surprise to him. He just responded with grace. No games. Just a showering of unspeakable peace in the midst of the worse thing I'd ever encountered. I was totally helpless as I lay there unable to move, but hindsight has shown me that I was helpless five minutes before, five months before, five years before. I had forgotten how helpless I felt five years back when I surrendered my life to him. Things were going good, and even though our communication had broken down, I was confident that Jerry and I would connect again— we always had. We weren't poverty-stricken anymore. We were in good health with, to us, a near-perfect child. But I'd become self-contained. I didn't purposely set out to nudge the Lord from my life; it happened as I slowly let the other junk inch in.

And now the turmoil that just moments before raged in my soul like boiling water, flew like a mist in the wind. And time, that accumulation of measured existence that demands that we race from event to event, that chronological stretch in the rhythm of our lives that we chop into organized segments, froze in a peaceful lull. True repentance washes away all previous sins, opens your eyes to the realization of God's presence, and causes you to enter into his rest. I was limp and helpless, but I had found my place of repentance. It didn't have to be that way. I could have repented without lying bruised and mangled in the floor of an automobile, but thankfully, I was spared life to do so.

Not everyone is so fortunate. And having these years to study the word, I see strife as the doorman to every evil work. The Lord was as near as my heart's beckon, not just that dark Friday, but every day. There's no ocean deep enough, no fire consuming enough, no war cold enough that he cannot hear his name, if only in a thought. Sometimes we find ourselves in a dark place, even though the sun is shining all around. It can be so lonely there that your skin dries and scales like a fish and your eyes hurt from lack of moisture. Fear can paralyze you to the point of incapacitation, and the hole you find yourself in seems to have no exit. But if you'll dare to whisper that name—Jesus—a glimmer of light will seep through and hope will form a solitary bubble in your soul. You don't have to be lying helpless in a crumbled mass of metal—I've been there and never left the house. The point is: he met me where I was, and he'll meet you wherever you are if you'll call on his name.

Jesus may have sent it via an angel, or he may have delivered it by his Spirit, but the gift of grace for my immediate need saturated my being with an unearthly balm. It was the grace that his death at Calvary procured for that day and time. I've tried since to recapture it, that unheard music that soothes the soul in the midst of trouble, but it was dispersed for the occasion, measured for the need. I would think that such an uncanny peace would be out of the ordinary for one who thought death might be staring her in the face, but I like to believe that this kind of peace is reserved for the children of God. After all, we may not like the process, but Psalm 23 tells us that death, for those who know Jesus as Shepherd, is just a shadow, and a shadow never hurt anyone. In the natural, I could have easily gone into shock, but the Holy Spirit was my shock absorber! The enemy tried to steal more than my four limbs that day; he tried to rob me of the chance to watch my tow-headed shoot'um-up-bang-bang develop into the wonderful man he is today. He tried to smother experiencing the love of a chocolate-eyed brother, who in some ways has been more like a son than a sibling. And if the enemy couldn't end our marriage by taking me out, he had plenty more tricks up his sleazy sleeve.

Yes, I've asked more than a few "whys," pondered a million "what-ifs." But I'm none the wiser. Through the years of learning about the nature of God, I have decided that to chide him for bad things in our lives does not mirror the word. To say that God needs tragedies to accomplish his work through us is to say that Calvary failed. That's about all I've learned as to the "whys" and "ifs." And that's probably enough until I make it home. The fact followed by question is: It happened, and am I praising God anyway? Am I allowing his Holy Spirit to use it in some positive way? I believe God takes pleasure in turning bad things around and working them for our good and his glory. To deny him that opportunity by harboring bitterness would be like stunting my own growth. How can the branch live if not connected wholeheartedly to the vine? Doesn't the stem bleed when a flower is broken?

One thing's for sure: The reflection I perceived as adequate in the full-view mirror in our bedroom the night before the accident needed work on the inside. I shutter to think how far I might have strayed before looking up had I not been forced to lie flat on my back. I don't have an explanation for everything that transpired, but I know I will understand it all in heaven some day. And even then, when I'm just like Jesus, there will be a marked difference: My glorified body won't have any scars—his will.

As for mine and Jerry's marital problems, as the film rolls you'll see that apologies slide easily off lips tallowed by the possibility of love forever lost. In my mind's eye, I see an angel hovering over the two of us as reality douses cold water in our faces. Can't you see him, strong and angelic, guarding us with a somber expression?

Wait just a minute. Wait one cotton-picking minute! What does he think he's doing? Oh man, he's on his knees. And his wings are inverted beneath his quivering angel chin. Well, the nerve of him. He's begging for another assignment!

# 3

# YOU CAN'T GET AWAY
# FROM GOD'S LOVE

*Who shall separate us from the love of Christ? Shall tribulation, or distress, or persecution, or famine, or nakedness, or peril, or sword?* —ROMANS 8:35

"IS SHE STILL ALIVE?" a husky voice shouted from somewhere amid the trees and rubble. *Alive?* I wondered what the man who was reaching through the broken glass to gently stroke my head could see that I couldn't.

"Yeah," he hollered back. The conversation among those gathering around the wreckage cut into my tranquility like an alarm clock disturbs peaceful sleep, but there was no snooze button that I could push to delay what was happening. I was thankful for human presence, but their panic was slicing away at my peace, and in spite of my spiritual encounter, my brain told me I had a real mess on my hands.

"You're going to be okay," the man with the soothing hand said.

"But I can't feel…I can't move." Just speaking the words seemed to solidify the severity of the situation. And although I still felt cleansed and intimate with my maker, the warmth birthed in my spirit was pulverizing like layers of sand in the wind.

"Can you move anything?" he asked.

"No."

"Well, I'm going to stay right here with you until the ambulance comes…you'll be all right…just hold on." I tried to believe him.

"Who is it?" a distant male voice asked.

"Sandra Hobson…uh…used to be. Jake Hobson's girl," another man answered. *There are people out there who know me.* That thought brought a fleck of comfort.

"Anybody called the ambulance?" a man asked.

"Yeah, somebody's gone now," my friend replied. He continued to comb my hair with his fingers and, in his own way, reassure me that everything was going to be okay. Moments hung between chatter. I couldn't see the people, but their movements sounded like someone had turned up the volume in my ears: tires slowing down on the pavement, doors slamming, the rustling of fallen leaves, and acorns crushing beneath scurrying feet. Every breath my friend took was like the north wind. Sounds had never been so intense; one more notch and I could have heard their thoughts.

Finally someone shouted, "They're on their way."

"What happened?" another asked. The man who knew I was Jake Hobson's daughter began explaining what he saw. But the answer lay much further back than the details of the collision. Heavier thoughts squelched his voice from my mind. I knew whatever description he gave would only scratch the surface of the truth; the real catastrophe started when I stopped praying and started scheming. When I surrendered divine arms of protection for the lust of the eye. When I switched the station carrying the "The Gospel Hour" for Tammy Wynette's "D-I-V-O-R-C-E." When I pushed back the voice telling me to abide under the shadow of the Almighty and listened to the liar in my mind saying, "You're all right, just go with the flow."

The crowd grew quiet. A rush of desperation swept through me. "Would somebody pray?" I begged. It's amazing how quickly one can be humbled. I don't know how many heard me, or if anyone heard me. But if they did they must have thought I said, "pay" instead of "pray," because nobody spoke up. Maybe some were praying, but it would have been nice if they had let me know. At this point, though, I was grateful for what I could get. Their help, especially the touch of the stranger who was at arm's length, was giving me a measure of security. Sometimes God's hands move through humans. The man's touch held fear at bay until the ambulance service arrived.

"She can't move," my friend informed the ambulance crew of two.

"How you doing, Sandra?" I recognized Fred Phillips' voice.

"I can't move." I told him.

"Okay gal, you just hold on. Me and Richard are gonna get you out of there." Richard Huff and Fred Phillips were by no means strangers to the area. "Can you get that door open?" Fred asked Richard. He was working diligently to open the door on the driver's side.

"Nope, gonna have to prize it, too." Richard responded.

Fred's professional hands replaced the gentle hands of the stranger who was reaching through the broken glass on the passenger's side where I had been thrown on impact. "Sandra," you're gonna hear us forcing these doors open, but don't worry; we'll have you out in a second," Fred explained. Crowbars attacked the metal like a dentist digging for a tooth. The sound told me if anything was left of Daddy's car, it would soon be unsalvageable. By now, I no longer cared. My heart was in my neck, breathing was labored as dust seasoned the inside of the car, and the noise was gruesome. I just wanted out!

Finally, the door on the passenger's side screeched open. "You 'bout got it?" Fred asked. Richard didn't have to answer; it sounded like the door on the driver's side fell off the hinges.

"You still okay, Sandra?" Fred asked.

"Yeah," I replied. But I wasn't okay. I was, though, coherent and without pain.

"Now here's what we'll do: I'm gonna slide my hands under your head—you tell me if it hurts—and Richard will pick up your legs. When I count to three we're gonna lift you onto this stretcher."

I squeaked, "Okay," and then Fred's fingers wiggled their way under my head, clutching my cheek like a spider clutching a fly. He knew that one wrong move could take me out instantly.

"One, two, three," he counted. And then the carpet released my right cheek and warm blood trickled toward my nose like a muddy river running downstream. I never felt Richard's hands on my body as the two of them hoisted me onto the stretcher. Pain would have been encouraging at this point, but there was only the sting from the cut on my forehead. Fred and Richard were careful to keep me in the position in which I had fallen. I never saw a face during the whole forest adventure, just the moving ground, my left arm when it dangled off the stretcher like a limb falling from a tree, and then Fred's hand as he reached to place it neatly by my side. It was a chilling reminder that they were also our town's morticians.

The ride to the hospital was like a dream in slow motion from which I couldn't awake. Lying on my stomach with my head toward the window, I still could not see Richard as he dabbed my forehead with a cloth, but I had a one-eyed view of the Yadkin River and the maples that lined Conrad Road. I wondered why Fred didn't turn on the siren. *Maybe I'm not seriously hurt,* I told myself. Yes, I was sure that was it. He'd seen this before, that's why we seemed to be going so slowly. He knew this would wear off and I'd be home with my family talking about the excitement of the day. I'd tell them how God came with his forgiving balm as I lay in the floor of Daddy's wrecked car. I'd probably tell it several times. Feeling clean on the inside felt good. From now on life would be sweeter.

"Is Jerry at work, Sandra?" Richard asked.

"No, he's at his uncle's helping prime tobacco," I replied.

"Do you know how we can get in touch with him?"

"Call my daddy," I said, then recited the number. "Richard, why can't I feel anything?"

"I don't know, but we're almost to the hospital. Are you hurting anywhere besides your head?"

"No."

The ambulance eventually crawled to a stop, and I watched the feet of caretakers/undertakers dance with efficiency as Richard and Fred wheeled me through the doors of the ER at Forsyth Memorial Hospital in Winston-Salem.

"No feeling from the neck down," Fred spit out.

"Fred, don't leave me!" I pleaded, my eyes following his black wing-tips. I needed the comfort of familiarity.

"I'll stay till somebody gets here, hon, unless I get another call."

Once in a cubicle, hands that were neither warm nor cold flipped me like a pancake, and for the first time, I saw faces. My eyes squint-ed from the blinding light, then rumbaed from stranger to stranger as they teamed to act out their skills. The room smelled etheric, the air lacing my upper lip, frigid. They worked on my body routinely, as if I were incoherent, ignoring that my sense of reason was still intact. A dark-haired, thirty-something intern in a suit made out of the same stiff seaweed-colored cotton as the curtain that separated me from the next victim, searched my eyes with a small instrument with the curi-osity of a stargazer.

"How we gonna get this tight sweater off?" a nurse asked him.

Eager to prove I was not a cadaver, I inserted, "Cut it off!"

"Good idea," she said, then grabbed a shoe in each hand. Another nurse aided her in peeling my pants, hose, and panties from my body before cutting through the snowflakes on my sweater. The cold scissors felt like life against my upper chest and neck as she unfolded the turtleneck above my chin and divided it with her scissors. After the initial strip, I was covered with a sheet from the neck down and the usual interrogation began: name, date of birth, weight, height, marital status, number of pregnancies, last period, mother's maiden name.

"Hey, can we do this later? I can't move!"

"I'm afraid—"

"What's wrong with me?" I interrupted.

The intern stepped back in. "Mrs. Miller," he said, and then looked up from the chart. "Dr. Berkley has been called in to examine you. He's a neurosurgeon here, and he'll be able to answer your questions." But he knew, and so did the nurses. They knew what they saw, but they couldn't say it. Not to me, anyway. "You cold?" he asked.

How was I to know if I was cold? My body was trembling, but my largest organ—my skin—had closed down on me. Was it the temperature or the trauma making me tremble? "Yes, a little," I answered, and then he got a blanket out of a locker and covered me with it as if to say, "That's all I can do."

They darted in and out like busy ants, finishing the forms, shining lights into my eyes, and asking if I was warm for what seemed like an hour or more before the head nurse on morning ER duty entered and announced, "There's some people out here who are anxious to see you." A knot rose up in my throat at the thought of Jerry's presence. She pushed my gurney out into the hallway where he and Daddy anxiously waited.

Jerry leaned down over me. "Hey," he said softly. He didn't know what to do with his hands, which were sticky with black tobacco gum. That he desired to touch me was obvious. That I wanted him to, unmistakable. He scanned my face with his eyes, avoiding my limp body, then swallowed hard. "What happened?"

"The car wouldn't crank." My eyes glazed over like a melting pond. "So I got Daddy's." I blinked, and water spilled onto my face. "I was messing with the radio, and…" by then the sobs were too overt to be ignored.

The nurse who rolled me into the corridor intervened. "I'm sorry." She directed her words toward Jerry. "We've got to keep her calm." Then she addressed me authoritatively. "If seeing them is going to upset you, I'll have to take you back."

"No, no, please," I begged. "Please let my husband stay." I bit my bottom lip and forced the sobs inward.

She hesitated.

"Okay, but we've got to keep you quiet." She looked at Jerry's gummy hands. "Sir, you can wash your hands down this hall, first door on the right." Jerry nodded, and then followed her instructions like a scolded pup.

Daddy, who had been looking over Jerry's shoulder, stepped up as next of kin. By his expression, I could tell that a reprimand for carelessness wouldn't happen now, probably not ever.

With tears under semi-control, I said, "Daddy, call Phil, and let her know I won't be in today."

Daddy looked pale and distant, like he was in a dream where he had floated to the door of his bedroom in black and white polka-dotted boxers and handed me the keys to his car, and the next thing he knew, he was pulling his golf clubs out of a wreckage. "Uh, what's the number?" he asked.

He echoed the number I gave, then walked away to search for a telephone.

It was too early to contemplate that I might never again race over the speed bumps, jump from my Toyota, wave at the guard as I take the steps by two's, dash down the long walk and into the building, then slide into my workspace like a runner sliding home. Speed on my feet and with my hands was a God-given talent that I had spent a lifetime accentuating. Short people do that. Young people take for granted that they will do that forever. I had promised myself I would play basketball with any league that would have me until I was a snaggletoothed granny. Not because I wanted to prove something, but because I loved the game. I'd been jarred before. I always bounced back.

The nurse returned and pushed me into a room where I would wait until the doctor arrived. Jerry returned, took my hand in his, and our eyes, which had not connected in weeks, embraced. "I'm so sorry," he whispered. I understood his words to be an apology as much as empathy for my plight.

"Don't, it's over," I said. I knew he would try to assume all the blame for our problems, and my need for honesty couldn't allow it. It was all so trivial, so utterly silly, compared to this moment. The healing of emotions had clearly begun, but unfortunately, it was initiated by a cold slap of reality. Why do we pathetic humans do that to each other? If love is real, it should be expressed, not played with like a toy then stuffed back on a shelf. Jerry touched my face gently, where he knew I could feel. His lips brushed mine lightly and one solitary tear fell off his face onto my cheek. I wondered if he knew how much I loved him. How could he really know the depth of my love after the past night's escapade?

Dr. Berkley, a medium height, dark-haired man in his early forties, burst through the door and wasted no time. He introduced himself, and the man following him as Kirt Orman, his PA. "What happened?" he asked.

I began to explain, while he did his own search into my eyes. "I had a wreck on my way to work."

"Were you thrown out of the car?"

"No, but I fell. I can't move."

He picked up my right hand and sat my elbow on my stomach. "Try to move your arm," he said.

I couldn't.

He laid my right hand on my chest.

"Now try."

It moved slightly. A smile stretched across Jerry's face and mine answered it. We were grasping for straws, anything positive to cling to.

The doctor reached for a pencil-shaped tool in the pocket of his white jacket and started pricking my arms and hands with its pointed edge, his PA observing closely. "Tell me if you feel anything," he instructed.

But there was nothing, not even a flex.

Then he moved up and down my legs with his leadless pencil. Jerry and I hungered for a sign of normalcy like dogs waiting to be tossed some sort of treat.

Still nothing.

As Dr. Berkley challenged my reflexes, Jerry and I were stunned at my body's inability to respond. The two men didn't seem surprised.

*What happened, God? What on earth happened in that excursion with the pine tree to do this to me?* I was afraid to voice the question, but Dr. Berkley read my thoughts. "Sometimes the numbness wears off," he said. "It could be a whiplash from your neck being forced back and forth in the crash." He patted my arm and smiled warmly, then ordered an X-ray of my neck like one would order a cheeseburger.

It was business as usual for them; one more case of twisted fate. But for Jerry and me, the propagation of our lives being forever changed had yet to take seed. The power of God's love caressed my spirit with unspeakable peace immediately after impact. I found my place of repentance. I made peace with maker and mate, the latter being no small feat to the former.

God had fused Jerry and myself into one being in his sight on June 1, 1968. His will was for us to live in harmony with his Spirit and each other. But like so many, we rebelled, and according to I Samuel 15:23, *rebellion is as the sin of witchcraft, and stubbornness is as iniquity and idolatry.* Oh, we dwelled together, shared the same last name, and slept in the same bed, but our rebellion and downright stubbornness kept our hearts at arm's length.

I figured this rude awakening was a mission of some kind. And I was sure that since the mission was accomplished, it would come to a quick resolution and I'd soon be my old self again.

But I had things to learn, and my being in a hurry didn't seem to sway God's timing. I might have thought the mission was accomplished, but there was a little-girl spirit that needed to grow up, and a male-dominating spirit that had to be dealt with. No, I haven't changed my mind: God doesn't cause wrecks. He heals, sets free, and delivers. But I believe lessons can be learned from adversity. And I found out the hard way that humility is not learned overnight. If I could've learned it instantaneously, maybe I would have been healed instantaneously. But I sometimes prematurely close the door to learning, listening to my soul's heart, rather than the heart of my spirit. Contrary to popular lyrics, life is not always a cabernet, but it is laden with lessons!

Golden curls dangled freely, framing the young X-ray tech's face. Mine was one of many pictures she'd take before her weekend officially began. She yawned and positioned the huge camera over my head. With the tray-like cassette in one hand, she lifted my head with the other.

"Oh God! My neck!" I screamed. My reference to God's name wasn't something I threw around frivolously; I'd been taught better. No, this exclamation was a cry of desperation as a sting shot through the back of my neck like a bullet. It was my first experience with real pain—a premiere of what vertebra crushed like mush could generate.

She lowered my head quickly. "I'm so sorry," she apologized. "Will you be all right until I can get some help?"

I squeaked out a yes, but there on that narrow table, during those brief moments alone after my first episode with pain, a feeling I had never before encountered flooded my emotions. My head was the only part of my body I could successfully govern, but it was weighed down by a hundred plus pounds of flesh and bones—body parts that required my brain to join forces with a trillion nerves before they could function. But that union of forces had been horribly severed. I had never felt this out of control, as if the X-ray technician didn't return promptly, some unidentifiable force would roll me off that table and I'd splatter guts and sinew from here to yon.

Through salty tears, I saw the figure of a man standing to the left of me. He seemed to appear from nowhere. Was he an angel, the death angel, maybe? I blinked, then recognized him to be Dr. Berkley's PA. I wondered about the pink scar that covered most of his cheek. He bore the presence of one who had learned compassion through experience and had gained credentials because of his need to exhibit that compassion. He pulled a handkerchief from his back pocket and wiped my nose like a father would a child, folded it, then dried my face. "Thanks," I whispered. He replied with a smile, and then with the professional hands that had just wiped my nose, he lifted my head, allowing the shaken X-ray technician to slide the cassette under my head without more trauma to my neck.

But a demon I had never encountered found a foothold. Fear can seem like a monster. It is fashioned in degrees and uses the victim's circumstances as credentials to invade precious territory, slowly tightening its grip until it chokes the victim's ability to reason. In my opinion, knowledge is the greatest defense against fear, but at that stage, I had none.

Maybe Kirt Orman *was* an angel. I never told him, but something beyond the call of duty radiated from his presence. I may have had him pegged all wrong; maybe I just wanted him to view me as a person and not an object of his profession. But as he stood day after day in the shadow of Dr. Berkley and Dr. Wingard, and joined the many profiles looking down at me in the months to come—some teaching, others learning—he brought a sense of warmth into my room. He wasn't much for chit-chat, but Kirt Orman made me feel as though I had the potential of a well-groomed racecar right before the checkered flag, when a more realistic comparison would be a wounded pile of body parts plugging toward pit row. And he mostly accomplished this with his soft touch, tender eyes, and calming smile.

I was a long way, though, from realizing that an evil spirit had just invaded me, and that the new faces in the medical field would be regular visitors in the weeks ahead. Once the X-rays were completed, the technician rolled me back into the small room in the ER, where I lay silently contemplating the pain I'd experienced in my neck and what it could mean. The hum of gurneys trafficking the halls with the precious cargo of human lives and the clank of care being administered reverberated as a backdrop to my pondering. Amid the shuffle, a nurse with the signs of ER fatigue entered carrying a sterile white collar. She slipped it routinely around my neck, and then announced, "You can go home now."

"Go home?" I echoed. "I can't even move!"

"Sorry, wrong patient," she apologized, bringing her shoulders to her chin as she backed out the door. I was glad she hadn't administered any medication!

The morning had yielded to afternoon before Jerry followed my gurney to the first available room on the fourth floor. "You're welcome to use the empty bed if you want to stay with your wife tonight," the head nurse told him. "She'll be transferred to a private room as soon as one comes available." It was a relief to hear that Jerry could stay the night. The thought of being alone without being able to lift a finger was bone chilling. I remember thinking once, as my fingers danced across my keyboard at work, that I'd be in bad shape if I couldn't use my hands. At the time, I couldn't imagine what that would be like. Now I knew, and "bad shape" didn't adequately describe it.

I had risen at the beginning of the day with the expectation of life as usual: Go to work, enter some information into a machine, drive thirty minutes home, and enjoy the weekend. But instead, my favorite sweater was in shreds, an I.V. was feeding me, a bag hanging off the bed served as my portable bathroom, and someone else was putting my six-year-old son to bed.

Lines of fatigue etched across Jerry's forehead like wrinkles in a slept-on sheet. He was studying the floor at the foot of my bed when Delta Bean arrived. Although Delta had turned forty and I was only twenty-six, we had become good friends at work; she was like the word walking into my room. I didn't waste any time asking her to find the Gideon Bible in the drawer beside my bed. The last thing on my muddled mind that morning was listening to someone read scripture verses, but the world around you looks different when the only way you can look is up.

"What would you like for me to read?" Delta asked.

I didn't hesitate. Romans 8 was what I needed to hear. I knew what it said, but I needed to hear *If God be for us, who can be against us?* It may not have been what the doctor ordered, and I can't say that I understood it all, but hearing *If the Spirit of him that raised Jesus from the dead dwell in you, he that raised up Christ from the dead shall also quicken your mortal bodies by his Spirit that dwells in you,* was better than a blood transfusion. And the portion that reads *If he spared not his own Son, but delivered him up for us all, how shall he not also freely give us all things?* seemed uncommonly reasonable. Just knowing that not even *tribulation, distress, persecution, famine, nakedness, peril or sword* could separate me from the love of Christ, and that neither my *life,* my *death,* nor this sudden inability to function could sever his all-powerful, all-knowing existence in my life gave me the leverage I needed to hold on. When you allow the word to take preeminence over your circumstances, a settling of mind and spirit takes place that drives fear away so God can work. I knew that God was with me, just as he had always been: watching, wooing, and drawing me to worship. I sucked the words Delta read into my spirit like a newborn at her mother's breast. A life of church and Sunday school had taught me about God; I had received his redemptive work. Now I was having to trust him for more—my hands, my feet, and everything in between.

The countenance of the man at the foot of my bed whose worst worry the previous night had been a chafing wife who wouldn't let him enjoy Lit'l Joe's capers in peace, now grimaced with disbelief in the present and trembled with fear for the future. And although spiritual things had not been precedent in an outward way, Jerry, too, was pierced with the promise of hope that only God's word can bring.

Later that night, the fourth-floor second-shift workers departed and another shift was briefed on new arrivals. I swallowed a handful of pills, but not even the Valium could buffer the trauma of the eventful day. Only the sustaining promise of God's unchanging love and our renewed love for each other kept us from totally losing it.

And, of course, our unseen angel.

An occasional snore from Jerry in the adjacent bed let me know that at least one of us was seizing bouts of sleep between thermometers shaking, bags being emptied, and intercoms blasting. But when his lanky body spilled onto the floor in the wee hours of the morning, the startle evoked a duet of laughter in spite of our adverse circumstances. Somewhere in the third heaven the all-seeing eyes of the God who created humor must have rolled upward at this display of angel antics. Thank God he shares them with us when we need them most.

And I thank God that in a room on the fourth floor of a hospital in a southern city, amid the shaken lives of a young couple, the love of God reigned strong and undeniable. And just because he could, I think he peeked sixteen years into our future and prearranged a Sunday morning service where I would sing and give my testimony in Clemmons, North Carolina. I think he enjoyed whispering, "Remember her?" into a man's ear—a man who just happened to be visiting that church on that particular day. A few questions from him at the end of the service verified that he was indeed the man stroking my head through the broken glass after the accident. Finally, through tears of joy, I got to thank him.

That's just like the Lord to tie things together and bring us full circle somewhere down the road. But like most, I've spent countless nights watching the clock tick the hours away, while wondering why things didn't change. It's when I try to reason things out with my intellect based on my senses that I lose faith and become frustrated. Only faith in God's infallible word strengthens me to press onward. It is the word that I must trust when all else fails. For I am persuaded that *nothing* can separate me from his unchanging love.

# 4

## M A M A

*Thy mother is like a vine in thy blood, planted by the waters; she was fruitful and full of branches by reason of many waters.* —EZEKIEL 19:10

IT'S 11:30 P.M., SUNDAY, October 5, 1975—day three of what is turning into a private hell. Nothing has changed; the only positive thing to report is that I'm breathing and functioning from the neck up. I wouldn't know until later that I scarcely eluded a tracheotomy, or how fortunate I was to have escaped head injuries. The hospital halls are quiet now, except for the periodic intrusion of the intercom summoning doctors to duty, clipboards clanging, and an occasional chuckle from the nursing station.

I've been promoted to room 406—a private room at the end of the south wing. I've had my sponge bath, a handful of pills, enough cranberry juice to keep a small ship afloat, and a cup of prune juice as a chaser. My liquid intake and output chart hanging on the inside of the door looks impressive. So far I've been a good patient.

Hazel, my private-duty nurse for the night, is reclining, hoping to catch a nap before she has to turn me again. But an hour is a long time to lie in one position when you can't move. It doesn't matter that your skin has no feeling, after a while you feel like your bones are in a pile; you simple have to turn.

Seven pounds of weight branch like antlers from the two holes Dr. Berkley made in my head on Saturday. No numbing, no anesthesia; he just mowed the hair away, then drilled for gold.

Dr. Berkley explained that the scalp is made to endure a lot, which makes sense—God chose that location for the brain. And as it turned out, the procedure was not as bad as it sounds. I found I was hard-headed, literally.

By Sunday, the indentations in my partially shaven head, where the Crutchfield Tongs are inserted, have become irritated. The grease the nurses are dabbing around the area brings only temporary relief. But I don't care about my semi-bald head, or that I resemble an alien. I want this nightmare to end. I want my husband. My baby. My life.

And I want my mama.

\* \* \*

At home Mama—"Sissy" to her two brothers, "Sis" to her friends, "Ruth" to Daddy, and "queen of sales" to her colleagues—pulls her white-and-tan Maverick slowly into their one-car garage. At forty-four she's still a size seven, and Clairol helps keep her short, fine hair a golden blonde. Skin care has been a priority since she started working for Keller Cosmetics after Mark was born. Ruth means beautiful, and the name fits.

I did not inherit her skin tone or dark eyes: I'm fair and blue-eyed, like some other relative who slipped a gene through, but I've always admired blondes with brown eyes. I've teased her about her Bob Hope nose until she's become self-conscious. We've always compared our-

*Ruth and Jake Hobson.*

selves like sisters instead of mother and daughter with plenty of kidding about our imperfections. When I was very pregnant and wearing Jerry's underwear, the two of them laughed at me until I cried.

On the night at hand, Mama is exhausted from an active weekend spent at a cosmetic convention in Nashville, Tennessee. She just wants to unwind and make it to bed. The absence of Daddy's LTD this late at night leaves her with the assumption that he's already left to pull third shift at the plant. She figures nine-year-old Mark is safely tucked in bed at her in-law's house, and the trailer next door holds her sleeping daughter, son-in-law, and grandchild.

She grabs the bag holding her cosmetic essentials from the backseat and decides the rest can wait until morning. The way she feels, maybe early afternoon.

*Odd,* she thinks, as she steps into the breezeway, *it's not like Jake to leave a light on.*

The door leading to the kitchen is unlocked. Something doesn't feel right. A flashback of her dad's first heart attack the last time she took a business trip sends a shockwave through her body. She turns the knob, and then pushes the door open with her bag.

Daddy's sitting straight—too straight—in the beige fake-leather chair at the far end of the den and kitchen combo. He's fully dressed except for his shoes, and he looks pale—too pale.

The TV's reporting the eleven o'clock news, but his eyes are not on the box—they're waiting to meet hers. Her heart hammers against her chest. She's no longer sleepy. Her eyelids widen in anticipation for an explanation for the deviation from his routine. What news was he waiting to tell? She doesn't wait for a greeting. She lowers her purse and night bag to the linoleum.

"Why aren't you at work?"

A moment of silence, as if he's lost the words he'd been preparing for the last hour, chills the atmosphere of their rural home like an evil presence.

"Sandra's in the hospital; she's been in a wreck."

\*   \*   \*

It's midnight when the door to Room 406 hurls open. My intensified sense of smell picks up the aroma of her presence like a honeysuckle breeze on a summer day. Daddy made the decision not to notify her of the accident before she got home. He knew what pushing her panic button was like. We agreed that he should wait until she was in the security of familiar surroundings to give her bad news, and that it would most likely be Monday morning before I'd see her. But in spite of the midnight hour and the violation of visiting-hour rules, her entrance came as no surprise.

You see, my mama is a golden retriever at heart, but she can be a real bandicoot: small framed, little head, pointed nose, known to be destructive, and carries her young in a pouch near her heart. At times she's a cross between a heckler and a badger: feeding at night, questioning by day. She is sly like a weasel and just as evasive when you're probing her for information.

She enters my room with Daddy's sister, Bernice, trailing her like a human pillow in case she toddles. Mama is dabbing her brown eyes speckled with flakes of gold with a Kleenex. The ride to Winston-Salem in Bernice's car gave her time to reflect on giving me life. She touches my arm gently, hoping I can feel her touch if no other. I tell her everything is going to be all right, and since she's here, I believe it will.

What she sees tells her otherwise. She wishes she'd been here, but what could she have done to change things? It's a natural instinct for a mother to take charge when her young is threatened. It's that mother's-love thing we accentuate on special occasions. Even when mother and daughter go through stages like two cats in a barrel, it's there—that unspoken bond linking you eternally. Your differences may fetor the air for a season, but your yoke with her is like a birthmark: permanently stamped in the womb.

Although in many ways you're alike, you will have some differences—your father's genes will see to that. You'll see black when she sees white. You'll roll your eyes at the dress in the department store that she's sure is "you." You'll throw up your hands when you exhaust every logical, but futile, way to prove a point. You cringe when you realize you've just stepped over the permissible line of expression, and duck instinctively when she raises her hands. But that unseen thread remains intact, woven too deeply to be unraveled by temporary lapses of sanity.

Later, when the shock lessens and the chill of reality sets in, she corners a doctor in the hall and demands that he tell it like it is. She needs to hear him say that her child will eventually return to her old self, flaws and all. It's okay if he says it will take a year, two years, or a decade. Just as long as he says there is a chance it will come.

But he can't paint a hopeful smile and say the words her ears long to hear. A brush off would be crueler than the truth, so he says, "I'm sorry, your daughter has a broken neck. Don't expect her to ever walk again." He leaves her with the word "never" reverberating off the corridor walls like the eerie echo of a haunting dream.

But he doesn't know *this* mother, or the bulldog grit, familiar only to those closest to her. Like a built-in protective mechanism, it erupts with the fervor of a volcano, culminating into a rope of hope that she clutches with ironclad fingers.

Doctor or no doctor. Broken neck or broken dreams. She'll not accept his prognosis. Not now. And knowing her, not ever.

But men are by nature pragmatic creatures. So when Daddy, poor guy, told her they'd might as well get my old room ready for when I came home, he meant well. He figured Jerry would eventually make himself scarce, that it would be too much for him to handle. But he should have known what he'd set himself up for—he'd faced this bulldog before.

Weakened by his own pain, his guard was down when she charged him for the counter-attack.

With the fire of determination burning in her eyes and the ardor of a junkyard dog her nose met his as she growled, "Don't you ever let me hear you say anything like that again! She will walk again! Do you hear me? Sandra will walk again!"

He might have thought it, but Daddy never said anything like that again. At least not in Mama's presence.

*      *      *

I believe mothers have special links to the Almighty, for only a mother can believe for the impossible when it comes to her children. Only the God-given instinct of a mother can reach beyond the stars into a place known only to the creator and find the unflappable determination to believe he will customize something supernatural because he understands the bond between mother and child. She was, after all, the vehicle he chose to bring this being into the world.

It seems reasonable to me that, with the exception of instances beyond her control, a woman who does not feel a nurturing responsibility toward her offspring (which age rarely alters) has, in some way, tampered with the laws of nature. I guess in some cases that inbred love means placing the fruit of her womb into the more-capable hands of another. Only God knows the heart. Only he can adequately judge.

And only God can knead a miracle from love texturized by adversity and moistened by a mother's tears.

Only God and Mama.

# 5

# DISTANCE CLEARS THE VIEW

*For now we see through a glass darkly, but then face to face; now I know in part; but then shall I know even as I am known.* —I CORINTHIANS. 13:12

GEORGE FERRIS DID me no favor when he invented his famous wheel. I mean, swinging seats suspending from a revolving wheel towering high above the housetops—really! I never did trust it—squeaking and swaying in the wind like a dizzy bird. It's holy terror for someone teetering toward acrophobia. Roller coasters, on the other hand, tickle a spot in the pit of my belly, causing an eruption of giggles to splatter through my body, which in turn, produces this gravity-forced, ear-to-ear grin. The climb is unnerving, but the tight-fitting bar and the arm of the person beside you give you security as you anticipate the thrill of the sudden fall.

Unfortunately, a roller coaster was not included in the convoy that set up camp at East Bend's tiny fairground for a week every autumn when I was a kid; the Ferris wheel was the center attraction. And of course, I couldn't allow my friends to sense my fear, so I'd risk my life for the sake of my reputation and climb into a rattling seat and pray that it wouldn't stop me (and whomever) on the top. But as sure as the maples swayed with fiery brilliance in the autumn breeze, the wheel would screech to a halt with me frozen slap dab on the top to let another sucker board below.

After a few laps, I'd muster the nerve to open my eyes so I could get a bird's view of people throwing darts, picking up ducks (my favorite), and pitching nickels into plates that weren't worth two cents. Each time the wheel circled, lifting me high above the shabby buildings and brown canvas tents, I'd make my discoveries: what boy was talking, walking, or riding with what girl—information to squirrel away for later gossip sessions with my friends. You know, girl stuff.

Since everyone in town knew each other, a guy talking to a girl who wasn't that girl's "regular" made juicy telephone conversation. Anything slightly suspicious had potential, but if you were lucky enough to actually spy handholding or a stolen kiss, you had some bona fide news. Distance really cleared the view.

Like the Ferris wheel, time has a way of elevating you to a place where, if you dare, you can see things from a different perspective. Trusting God for the ride is not always easy, especially when you're flitting through the air without wings. In the midst of what seemed like the beginning of the end for me, I can (now) see my tribulation belonging to the whole family, resulting in a pulling together of individuals as they dealt with their own grief.

Adversity never affects only one. My family members' unity became channels of strength for them in the weeks to follow, as well as myself. I'm resolved to the fact that I won't get all the answers to my questions while I'm on this earth, and since questioning keeps me hung in the past, I try not to sink back into those moments of despair. But the replay of my life's film has helped me get a broader picture. I believe God wills to reveal sense to our chaos, but we must learn to wait until things level out and our heads stop spinning before we can see the whole picture. For a "lion personality" like myself, the wait is not always easy.

If those nearest me had divided during this difficult time in our lives, I'm convinced it would have proven detrimental to my overall healing, as well as theirs—they had some serious life alterations themselves. At the time, my own suffering was too consuming. Time has helped me enter into their pain.

As I lay in Room 406, as dependent physically on the mercy of those around me as the day I was born, all I saw was my grim circumstances and the sense of helplessness on the faces of the people I loved. Legs burning like simmering coals from the bone to the skin intensified my yen for narcotics to transfer me to a land where dreams were more favorable than reality. Most of the time sleep was my only relief.

Inducing sleep required shots in the hip, but I didn't mind them because paralysis deadened the sting. So like an addict in need of a fix, I relied on the shots as buffers for the cruelty of consciousness.

My doctors could give no real explanation for the coming and going of the fire in my legs. "It could be feeling returning," Dr. Berkley said. That was an omen I could live with. Although I couldn't feel the towels soaked in ice that my legs were wrapped in like a mummy when the fire was unbearable, it seemed to help.

Why could I feel the torment raging under my skin and not the nettle of icy towels pressed against my legs?

God only knows. There never seemed to be a black and white explanation for my peculiarities.

I imagine nerves as long, thin soldiers stretching through swamps of blood and mountains of muscle on a mission. Like the spreading of a root they tread toward their destinations, fed by a god-like fluid hidden in a mysterious tunnel that science has yet to totally define. Even war scarred, nature equips them to try, whether successful or not, to reach the organs awaiting their crucial messages. I could not hate my nerves for their missed targets; I chose, instead, to believe the fire was friendly warfare.

Keeping my soul uplifted was another thing altogether. Sudden loss of everything from the neck down doesn't exactly bring with it a daily dose of cheer. And trust me, lying in your feces until someone gets around to cleaning you up is a humbling experience. I was convinced that my hair, the human oil can, had things growing in it. One cannot appreciate water from a shower running from head to toe until it is no longer possible, or the torment of an itch you cannot scratch. Peeing in a bag is not so bad as long as they don't let it run over, but I can't say that the hooking up process is all that pleasant. To watch my muscles, once firm and active, sag from the slow death of inactivity was in itself enough to depress the most optimistic soul. So sleep became my scapegoat, and I dared the "normal world" to defy me the pleasure.

I refused to look in a mirror for the five weeks I was in traction. Not seeing the "now" me helped preserve the image of the me I couldn't admit was gone. Unfortunately, others didn't have that advantage. The first visit I received from the elderly man who was presently the pastor at the church I attended was rudely revealing. "My," he said, gaping at me through honest eyes, "you look awful!" Well, that blew all the "you still look good" platitudes right out the window. Why would I even care at that point about how I looked? If you're a woman, I won't have to answer that.

I finally stopped asking for the stun gun when people started commenting about my mustache. A little inquiring traced the shots in the hip as the culprit. Too many male hormones, I guess. At least I could control my chances of being called the bearded lady in Room 406, but it meant dealing with reality for longer periods.

I remember praying on more than one occasion while driving to work that God would cause something to steer Jerry's attention my way. It was a misguided prayer, for I'd pictured myself laid out in an ivory bed like Snow White with Jerry hovering over me like a handsome prince. Of course, the scenario had a fairy-tale ending.

The God-created imagination, as wonderful as it is, can also be a diabolical entrapment if left to wander. When lived out, the grass on the other side of an untamed imagination can come back to haunt you. No wonder the word admonishes us to *cast down vain imaginations* (II Corinthians 10:5).

On the other hand, we *should* envision ourselves as healthy and prosperous. God saw Abraham as the father of nations when he was childless and too old to tango. It is not denial to make a choice *to speak those things that be not as though they were*. Abraham believed God and it was counted unto him for righteousness. Faith, like a muscle, needs exercising. And take it from one who has tried it both ways: Too much world and too little word causes faith to fizzle.

In spite of my past ignorance to unleashed imaginations and prayers lacking substance, from a distance I can see my family working around me like busy ants to make me as comfortable as humanly possible. They put their lives on hold, literally. I was no Snow White, but I see myself as the working point from which a silky web of unity was being woven as they reported for duty day after exhausting day. And I see them loving me even though my head was an oil berg with antennas and my bed a toilet.

Until pulled together by catastrophe, I don't think we really understood what being "close" meant. We were a typical small-town family, Jerry, Kip and I living next door to my parents and Mark, who lived next door to Grandpa and Grandma Davis, my maternal grandparents. Grandpa and Grandma Hobson, Daddy's parents, lived a couple of miles up the road. And Jerry's parents lived about eight miles away (as the crow flies). Hennis Freightline transferred Jerry's dad to

Spartanburg, South Carolina before I had the wreck, but they kept their homestead and traveled back on weekends.

Although Kip and Mark, being close in age and partners in grime, kept the path clean between our connecting yards, we adults had very little time to interact with our jobs taking us in different directions. Some weeks I only saw my parents at church on Sundays. My working hours were odd, and Mama traveled at night holding make-up classes. Grandpa Davis once commented that he saw more of Jerry *before* we got married. Funny, I felt the same way. And my parents had yet to bond with him. Like I said before, we were two dizzy-headed kids when we married; I blame many of our "brainless" choices on immaturity, number one being marrying too young.

Now the three of them (Jerry, Mama, and Daddy) had formed an around-the-clock vigil at Forsyth Hospital. They talked, shared feelings, and cried together. Jerry's parents, Troy and Gladys Miller, and his sisters, Ann Gentry, Linda Hutchens, and Jeanette Livengood, filled in when they could to give them a break. Ann and her husband, Tony, made space for Jerry and Kip in their home, even though they had two small children. Ann took Kip under her wings and saw to it that his school needs were met. I never worried that he wasn't being loved and cared for. But I did worry about the affect of so much change at such a young age. Kip told his first-grade teacher that if people would pray for his mama, she would get better. Oh that we all could have the faith of a child! His faith has pulled me out of many dark pits.

Jerry was granted a five-week leave of absence (without pay) from the textile plant where he worked as an electrician. When the big round clock on the wall in my room read 8:00 a.m., Jerry faithfully walked through the door, and Jessie Myers—my special night-time angel—would leave. It seemed as though Jerry and I were together more now than before the accident, but it was certainly a different kind of togetherness. And for the first time, we were really communicating. I watched God mellow Jerry like a pear in the noonday sun as the days crept into weeks. His whole demeanor changed. Having him by my side those first five weeks after my injury was worth more than any amount of money. He knew what every gesture meant, when I needed to talk, and when I just needed to rest. He turned me, positioned me, feed me, and held my hand through the toughest hours. He was a rock.

Jerry connected with a pastor from a neighboring church who dropped by two or three times weekly. Clyde Phillips was a short, balding fellow whose zany personality fit the aperture for the light Jerry needed. He was sensitive to Jerry's need for camaraderie with someone who could mentor him without judging. Clyde knew when to lay the scriptures out like a deck of cards and when to fold'um and crack a knee-slapper. He took Jerry out to eat occasionally to give him a break from the monotonous smells and sounds of hospital life. He brought Jerry a King James Bible, and reading it brought Jerry comfort as he fell asleep many nights between promises. Jerry and Clyde bonded like two beagle pups.

Deer hunting lost its spark for Jerry that season. Instead, he was the valuable game being stalked by the one who scopes the earth for those desiring to know him and his unconditional love. Jerry's heart was tenderized by the weeks of pounding on his topsy-turvy world. As he looked at my lifeless limbs day after day, fear of a future with a wife who needed constant care would only be normal. But not once did he show signs of defeat. His kisses were as passionate and satisfying as ever, maybe more. And a strength he'd never before needed held him up when images of escape flashed though his mind and fear and fatigue towered over him like an unclimbable mountain. He was easily won.

You think when your heart is so tender and you're lying prostrate at Jesus' feet that you'll never stray. Jerry will be the first to tell you that he has strayed over the years. As a matter of fact, he'll be the first to tell you that so have I. Painting a picture of two super saints would be a lie—that's not what this story is about. It's about a God of second chances—as many as it takes. In spite of our temporary lapses of good sense, Jerry made a heart change in 1975, and I'm satisfied his name was written in the Lamb's Book of Life in permanent ink. I fully expect to dwell with him throughout eternity. And for the record: I may not have been a beautiful princess, but my husband was more valuable to me than a thousand princes.

\* \* \*

Mama, the cosmetic queen, gave Jerry a break around lunchtime. Her lot fell to be my groomer: body massager (with her own special skin-softening concoction); facial specialist (never let it be said that

Ruth Hobson's daughter was deprived of proper skincare); nose pick-
er (I can still see her stretching her nostrils and saying, "Do like this");
and any other gross grooming need imaginable (mamas always get the
gross stuff).

Thanks to Mama (and natural oils), my skin had never been in better condition. When you only get sponge baths, your natural oils keep
you soft and pliable. But oh, how I longed to be hosed down! I day-
dreamed of someone kindly running a pitchfork through my hair.
Mama scratched my head with the same fervor she used to comb my
hair when I was little—like a dog digging for a bone. When I was
small, I would cry when she'd start toward me with a comb, and I've
got swollen-eyed pictures to prove it! Now, I craved her "tough hand."
Before the days of the herbal mask, Mama was known to be the community pimple excavator. I won't go into detail, but thank God I was
not an acne-prone adolescent or I might not be telling this story!

Despite her toughness, Mama is a classy, endearing lady. She just
knows how to grabble. And she can be (sometimes irritatingly) per-
sistent. But I admire her fearlessness. I've been with her to deliver cosmetics on many occasions and witnessed (from the car) giant, teeth-
showing, monster-like dogs follow her in hot pursuit all the way to the
front door. What does she do? With white cosmetic bag in one hand
and her purse swinging in the other, she says, "Shutcha mouth," and
never misses a beat.

But Mama carried her persistence too far on the day she set out to
cover up the smell of my greasy hair with a bottle of perfume she'd
smuggled into my hospital room. I abhor the smell of heavy perfume
under normal circumstances, and with my now intensified remaining
senses, smells were sharpened to the point of being torturous. But
dear ole Mom thought she'd pull one over on me. After all, how could
I retaliate? So she gets right up close to me and breaks out that perfume bottle like a revolver, getting in several shots to my head before
I can catch my breath enough to scream. And scream I did! Loud and
forceful! It was a sneaky trick, one I felt sure would prove fatal. There
I was, laid out like corpse, being attacked by my own mother. What
defense did I have save a hearty bellow? I can still feel the effects of
that smell today. Many moons have past, but I'm still waiting to catch
Sunshine Head when nothing is sticking out of the covers but a few
strands of golden fuzz. I'm going to sweeten them with something *I've*
concocted, and it won't be pretty!

You'd think one's own mama would understand one's peculiarities, but Mama repeatedly tried my patience. She was convinced that my room needed more light, that the sun coming in would cheer me. Wrong. Every time she'd unfurl the heavy gray curtains, my poor, sensitive eyes would go into shock. Only after a small tantrum would she give in and close the curtains.

Don't get me wrong; I am thankful for the senses God gave me. But only a person with abnormal sensitivity can relate. Take sound, for instance. Mama is a bubbly person, bent toward hospitality. If I had a visitor—and I always had a visitor—Mama felt compelled to entertain. After all, they had gone to the trouble to pay the parking toll and walk all that way to visit me, and I appreciated that, really I did. But on some days, whispers were like nails being hammered into my woodenhead. It's hard to explain how one can become so reactive to sensory stimuli overnight, and the only proof I had that I wasn't just a crybaby was my word. It went against Mama's grain to ask a guest to step into the hall, but that's exactly what Jerry did on several occasions. And those closest to me learned that if they didn't want me to hear something said, they'd better say it on another floor.

In many ways, I'm a lot like my mama, especially in mannerisms and appearance since I've aged. But in other ways, we are total opposites. I wish I had her patience; I want everything yesterday. I'm easily distracted, but she can tune stuff out, go on, and not let it bother her. I blurt out things like "Mama, you almost sideswiped that car!" She'll casually remark, "Yeah, but I didn't." Years ago she was shopping in a local clothing store when the adjacent store caught on fire. Everyone was panicking but Mama, who figured she had time to finish rambling through a table of sale items before the roof collapsed. Finally a flustered sales clerk hollered, "Oh Ruu-uth, the store's on fire!"

In spite of my quirks, which she labels "Daddy's genes," we became tight. During our time alone at the hospital, we conversed, and a gap that had divided us since my coming of age closed gently like the petals of a flower. Looking on the positive side of a bad situation, we had the chance of a lifetime to get to know each other as the women we had become. And in the process, we learned that love doesn't have to always see eye to eye.

Mama struggled to understand God's purpose in our sudden devastation. She lost her oldest brother when two planes collided during a flight maneuver in 1942. She was only twelve, but the memory of the day the telegraph came informing them of his death left wounds that she never totally recovered from; it wasn't fair to be going through another family crisis. Oddly, the one place that was unbearable for her was church. Our voices had blended in the choir since my childhood. We'd sung together in a church trio for several years. We learned instinctively when to switch notes. If her alto note was too high, then usually my tenor note was also, so she would drop and take my note an octave lower. So Sunday mornings became her self-designated shift on weekends. Some members couldn't understand why she wasn't in her place at church. They even volunteered to sit with me so she could attend. But the Lord understood, and he held her hand until she could walk through the church door again.

\* \* \*

The sound of Daddy's footsteps when he exited the elevator down the hall preceded him. His shift with me started when visiting hours ended at night and he stayed until he had to leave for work around eleven p.m. When you know someone so well, even his steps become identifiable.

It was not unusual to spot a flake of foil glistening on Daddy's face—he was a plant foreman at RJR Archer, an aluminum plant in Winston-Salem. I have his fair skin and temperament, but not his hair: a flattop then, still as black as night at forty-five. Daddy has this involuntary flinch on his upper lip, like someone has an invisible string tied to it, yanking it toward his nose every little bit. And there's this noticeable twitch in his shoulders. It makes you want to grab them from behind and scream, "Peace, be still!"

Mama never understood Daddy's twitch or his flinch, thought they were annoying habits he could control. But I understood, because I inherited the tendency to twitch and flinch, and I don't even realize I'm doing it. Like when I eat, if I'm not consciously trying to keep from it, I curl my upper lip. When I think about how silly I must look, I remember Grandpa Hobson's horse, Nell, and how she turned her lips inside out when my cousin and I fed her laying mash. Mark has some of the same tendencies, although he probably won't admit it. But I consider it kind of like your last name: a trademark showing you belong to the clan.

Daddy had his own passions about my immobility. Neither my

greasy hair nor its smell bothered him, but he was bent toward keeping my arms and legs moving. It had to be laborious. From the moment he arrived until he left he was pumping an arm or leg. And, of course, we had our conversations, too. I'd never felt I could talk freely to either of my parents, and since Daddy was a no-nonsense type of guy, we'd never before conversed for the pure pleasure of it. Television got on my nerves, seemed frivolous. I needed to hear something with substance. So when he was not pumping one of my four limbs, we talked or he read scriptures to me. If I didn't know better, I'd think the Lord planted me there to slow everybody down where we could focus on the more important things in life: God and each other.

There are many things that stand out in my memory of life (thus far) as Jake Hobson's daughter, but an elucidatory of life with the man probably wouldn't fill a canvas with exciting color. Except maybe the time when I was small and I painted his toenails red while he was asleep. He didn't notice them until he got to work and changed into his work shoes in front of several other guys. Or maybe the time I stayed up until he got home from working second shift to tell him that Mama and I had gone to a horse show with our neighbors and I had won a colt with a dollar raffle ticket. That was pretty exciting.

I was a daddy's girl from the start. The Sunday he walked down the isle and knelt at the old-fashioned altar to receive Christ is an image forever carved in my mind. I don't remember my age, but I couldn't have been over five or six. Daddy could do no wrong in my eyes, so if he needed a Savior, I was sure I did, also. He seemed upset to me, kneeling there with people crying and the preacher down on one knee with his arm around Daddy, praying out loud to God about him. So I started crying. Hard. That's when my aunt Bernice—the same person who escorted Mama to the hospital after the accident—got up from her planked pew and came to where I was on the far end of the front bench on the women's side of the church and wrapped her loving arms around me. I made up my mind right then and there if Daddy was going to be a Christian, so was I. A deeper commitment came later, but my prayers changed following that from the now-I-lay-me-down-to-sleep version Grandma Davis had taught me to actually talking to God from my heart about everyday things. And Daddy's getting saved stuck—from then on we were in church practically every time the doors were open.

I recall only one spanking from Daddy as a small child. We were at

Grandpa and Grandma Davis' house for Sunday dinner and I decided to sit in our car and pretend I was driving. The car was parked on a hill, and when I shifted the gear from P to D, it started rolling backward. Dumbfounded, I just sat there, holding tightly to the steering wheel. Luckily, Daddy and Grandpa were outside and saw the car headed swiftly toward the apple tree with my head barely detectable. "Put your foot on the brake!" Daddy yelled, as he chased the runaway car. I did, and the apple tree eluded a big bump. But my fanny didn't.

The other time was when I was in high school. I was sure he broke the *do not provoke your children to wrath* rule, but when I sassed him (not smart) he went outside, broke a small switch from a tree, and striped my legs good. Nothing could have hurt me worse, because I had visible red stripes for the next basketball game. But I thought twice before talking back to him. It was several moons before distance revealed to me that I was in the wrong on that call.

I've always been able to go to Daddy when I've been in a bind. Once, after a heated spat with Jerry when we were newly married, I threatened him by locking myself in the bathroom and crying, "I'll tell my daddy!" It worked, but I don't recommend it. Jerry's always had a lot of respect for Daddy. If we needed financial advice, I'd call Daddy at work; he seemed easier to talk to on the phone for some reason.

But from where I lay while he exercised my paralyzed arms and legs, I was listening more than talking, and he had a lot bottled up. He took me on a journey through his past, allowing old wounds to surface. I saw a different man emerge—a man whom under normal circumstances would never have been so vulnerable.

There's something about a good daddy that makes a daughter, no matter her age, still feel like a little girl. Since the beginning, I thought he could fix any problem. And even though he had a growl like a grizzly, I knew that beneath that persona was the heart of a teddy bear.

For the most part, I did a pretty good job of keeping my emotions intact. But on one particular evening, I hit rock bottom. Daddy had gone to his car to get something, and momentarily there was no one to hold up for or impress with demonstrations of faith and strength. In other words, no performance was needed. Solitude was something my family and friends had purposely kept me from. So alone for the first time, my emotions released like popping a balloon. During those intense moments, a floodgate opened and Daddy returned to find me trembling in a pool of despair.

Rattled, Daddy hurried to my side. "What's wrong?" he asked. I could only reach for him with my eyes. "I want to go home!" It was a futile plea for him to make everything better, like he always had. But for the first time in my life, Daddy's hands were tied. "You can't unring a bell," some wise person said. And Daddy couldn't beam us back to the morning of October third and refuse to give me the keys to his car.

That was the worst day during my hospital stay, and God only knows why Daddy had to be the one to deal with it. But even in the midst of my lowest encounter with grief, God was teaching me that it was time to switch fathers. It was a good school, but the tests were hard and the tuition high. As much as he wanted to, Daddy was limited to the powers of a human. Only my heavenly father could perform miracles.

*       *       *

Adversity has a way of pulling people together, and the web of unity holding us all grew tight as days passed. Leaning on the Lord was to our advantage, and he was most precious. Protecting me from the foreign agents of doubt and unbelief—which lurked like a contagious germ waiting to find a foothold—became this trio's focus. And I think heaven will affirm that they were successful: Jerry found the Savior. Mama became my friend. By faith, I released my earthly father of the impossible and recognized Jesus as my Abba Daddy.

Watching my parents embrace Jerry with a newfound admiration was a miracle in itself. Having a God-fearing family with unwavering support is worth more than the world and all its gold. I witnessed other patients who were deserted because a loved one couldn't handle the pressure. I consider myself blessed beyond description.

As the years roll, new obstacles arise that demand individual and corporate family faith to hurdle. Only as life lifts me farther from them and closer to the day when each of us will eventually reach the top of this not-always-so-merry ride, I'm confident we'll look back— fear forever gone—and with perfect vision behold that same Spirit that raised Jesus from the dead sustaining us through an ultimately victorious journey.

# 6

# PEBBLE BY PEBBLE

*For verily I say unto you, that whosoever shall say unto this mountain, be thou removed, and be thou cast into the sea; and shall not doubt in his heart, but shall believe that those things which he saith shall come to pass: he shall have whatsoever he saith.* —MARK 11:23

OUNTAINS TAKE my breath away. Like an artist at work, God paints the seasons with grandeur, while they quietly display their vast and unique beauty, compelling the eye to behold them. If mountains had souls, I'm sure they'd be tempted with pride. Carolinians enjoy the best of all four seasons, and living in the Piedmont, North Carolina, I'm strategically positioned at the foot of the beautiful Blue Ridge Mountains.

The Bible compares the trials in our lives to mountain climbing. The steep slopes challenge our fears. The rocky terrains reflect days when accomplishing the simplest tasks means persevering beyond the norm. I'm a strong believer in positive thinking, but I've never known anyone yet who has exercised enough faith to cause a literal mountain to take a dip into the sea. A flag goes up when I hear the phrase "mind over matter." We should be on guard to forces that are empowered by deception.

Yet Jesus told his disciples that if they had faith the size of a mustard seed, they could speak to a mountain and it would move. My intellect hasn't fully grasped that. I know we can't measure faith with a proverbial yardstick. People have made comments through the years that I've had "a lot of faith," but I want to hide under a rock when that happens. I do not claim to have great faith. I don't consider it boastful, however, to admit that faith was working in my life during this difficult time. How much was faith and how much was just stubborn determination? I do not know.

My definition of faith is: belief in a higher power to make something intangible tangible. And it's available to everyone who accepts the gift of Christ's atonement. If you try too hard to understand it, you're teetering toward nullifying it, because faith is not contingent upon the human senses or intellect. In other words, you can't figure it out like a math problem. Could that be why so many of the world's brilliant minds fail to embrace the simplicity of God's plan to interact with humankind?

Prior to the accident, I'd had some notable prayers answered, but I'd never needed a miracle healing of this magnitude. With natural reasoning, it would have been easier to yield to what medical people saw me as: a permanent quadriplegic. After all, they witnessed firsthand the result of injuries like mine every day. They saw the youthful expectations of a teenage boy crushed like the powder in the bullet that pierced his spine. The picture was forever etched in their minds of the young girl who innocently dove into shallow water and was pulled to the surface only to face a breathing tube and a life permanently scarred. There were no quick fixes.

When needing a miracle, we must dare to defy all logic, even to the point of being labeled a fanatic, if necessary. Chanting, "I think I can, I think I can" like the little locomotive won't give you enough steam. We're children of the light. We must stand on God's promises, recite them as we walk through the fire and tread through high waters, feast on them when food loses its appeal, and rest in them when sleep fails. Count on your righteous indignation annoying some, but realize there's too much at stake to cower at disapproval. I'm no stranger to phrases like "face reality" and "false hope" from well-meaning people. I've learned that skeptics often clam up when counteracted with, "But Jesus said…"

Call it what you will, but never taking another physical step was not an option I would let myself consider. There have been times, though, when I felt my faith was strong, yet I did not see the results I sought. Other times, I've seen miracles happen when I wouldn't have thought my faith could hold water. Many times, ignorance of what rightfully belongs to us hinders us from receiving. I like to find a scriptural reference for what I'm asking for, recite it to the devil, and then thank God that his word is true when everything else fails. As children of the King of kings and Lord of lords, we don't have to beg for what's rightfully ours. But we do have to receive it, and hopefully, with thanksgiving.

Proverbs 4:20–22 says, *My son, attend to my words; incline thine ear unto my saying. Let them not depart from thine eyes; keep them in the midst of thine heart. For they are life unto those that find them, and health to all their flesh.*

Likewise, Psalms 119:11 says, *Thy word have I his in mine heart, that I might not sin against thee.*

When I was in high school, my English teacher, Mr. Barns, required each student to stand in front of the class and recite a poem by heart. I memorized "The Road Not Taken" by Robert Frost, and kept it "in my heart" until my appointed time of recital. Did I know it the next week? Maybe. The next year? Possibly. Ten years later? No chance. I placed the words of the poem in my heart but I didn't renew my mind to them, so they slipped out of my consciousness with time. If we want to pass the tests in life, we must keep the word in our hearts. It may be the road less traveled, but when faced with adversity, it will make all the difference.

In the fullness of time, I'm sure we'll discover that the issue of faith is not as complex as religion makes it sound. After all, Jesus told his disciples in Matthew 19:14 to *Suffer the little children, and forbid them not to come unto me: for such is the kingdom of heaven.* Children don't struggle with faith, they simply believe.

Even though I was still a spiritual baby, faith was present in my life in 1975. I needed to hear my prognosis upfront, to know exactly what I was dealing with, so I asked Dr. Berkley point blank, "What can I expect?"

His curt reply was simply, "It looks bad." His countenance and the seriousness of his tone told me I should not push him to elaborate.

\* \* \*

Mama was at a cosmetic meeting in Charlotte, North Carolina, when Hazel Keller, owner of the company, walked up to her and said, "Ruth, tell your daughter to claim Mark 11:23." Mama grabbed a napkin off the table and scribbled down the chapter and verse. When she read it to me, I latched onto the verse as if it were written especially for me. She printed the verse on an index card and Jerry taped it to the parallel bar over my bed—right beside the Snoopy dog with the words "I love you" penned by his own hand on its belly. Both tokens were in constant view, and I needed the assurance they both brought.

Mark 11:23 became my covenant promise, belonging to me like a birthright, and it Scotchgarded my spirit from the negative energy perpetrating my room. When my intellect betrayed me with natural reality, Mark 11:23 was there like a faucet dripping heavenly honey on my wounds. I thank God for prompting Hazel Keller to share that verse with Mama; it was the best gift anyone could have sent me. And Hazel Keller being a prominent person in Mama's life reinforced the idea of claiming a particular verse for a particular need.

Prayers were going up for me everywhere. Only eternity will reveal them all. People who didn't even know me were standing as a proxy for me in their churches as hands were laid on them and they were anointed with oil. I had not yet been introduced to such practices, but I was grateful still. Cards and gifts flew in by coveys. I had never felt so loved. I didn't know how exactly, but I knew that by the grace of God I wouldn't remain in my present physical state.

\* \* \*

Unlike Dr. Berkley, whom I enjoyed joking with on a good day, Dr. Wingard sometimes displayed a gruffness that intimidated me. He was a tall, distinguished man with an accent. The nurses had told me that he had been notified by the White House when President Kennedy was shot. I never felt close enough to him to ask him if it were true, but he was definitely a man respected among his peers. The nurses also told me how he had gone into the solarium and wept after a young woman, just out of nursing training and newly married, had been brought in after an automobile crash paralyzed from the neck down. Up to this point, I had not seen his sympathetic side. I've never tried to hide the fact that I am as country as dirt, and my lack of formal education is sometimes daunting, so I may have been a little paranoid, but I sensed that Dr. Wingard associated my beliefs with weak mindedness.

The timing was bad for Dr. Wingard to make his rounds on the Sunday afternoon following Helen Church's visit. Memories of sitting in her tiny music room filled with memorabilia flooded my emotions. How she could make that Whirlizer ring! I was crying profusely after she left. As usual, Kirt Orman was with Dr. Wingard with clipboard in hand. Without a trace of mercy in his voice, the doctor commanded an explanation for my tears. "What are you crying about?" I simply replied, "My piano teacher just left." How could I explain in the five minutes he allotted me that my hands were still warm from her caressing the fingers she'd poured her soul into teaching the rudiments of church music? That her visit had resurrected the memory of how elated I was when I was fourteen and her husband, Scott, overheard a gospel song I was playing and thought it was she. That I was painfully aware that Bruce's death (her only child) from an automobile crash was still too fresh on her heart for her to be reliving it through me. I couldn't explain it, so I let him assume I was wallowing in the clutches of self-pity.

Dr. Wingard responded by tossing the sheet from my lifeless legs and pulling an instrument from the pocket of his surgical jacket.

"Do you feel this?"

"No."

"This?"

"No."

His lips were tight and his eyes fixed as he crept toward my thigh with his silver instrument. "How about this?"

I closed my eyes. "Uh, maybe a little," I responded.

He clearly didn't have time for maybes. "Why are you closing your eyes?" he stormed.

"It helps me to concentrate," I squeaked. But I was also trying to make my eyes hold the water that was leaking onto my face.

"Well, keep your eyes open, and tell me if you feel this or not."

"I think I do, a little, I don't know for sure," I said, while thinking: *Just get out of my sick room and leave me alone, you educated master of insensitivity!*

Disgusted with my uncertainty, he flung the sheet back over my once-active legs and muttered as he exited the hospital room, "You either feel it, or you don't." Kirt Orman trailed him like a monk following the Pope.

I'm still trying after twenty-seven years to articulate the weirdness going on under my skin. To what do you compare zigzagging sensations that charge to your heart like a bolt of electricity? Maybe it's like being struck with lightning, only sized down. Sometimes a touch on the outside ignites a spark on the inside and your nerve endings are the conduit carrying the flame that makes your heart itch momentarily. And then there are those "hot spots" you learn not to touch, like the place on my chin that makes a place on my left leg feel like my throat does when I think about a puppy licking me in the mouth. These weird sensations are not to be confused with the spasticity that has its on abnormalities—like the sudden stabbing pain in my hip that results in my leg jumping involuntarily like someone has hit my knee with a hammer. Touches I once enjoyed, like clawing the bottom of my feet, now tell my brain it hurts. After awhile, your body adjusts to the tingling, heart-itching sensations like swallowing or batting your eyes, but it was all too new at the time to decipher.

\* \* \*

It was determined that an anterior effusion of my fourth and fifth cervical vertebra was necessary. Dr. Holms, an orthopedic surgeon, would remove a chip of bone from my left hip to be used to fuse the vertebra. A small incision would be made on the front of my neck, about and inch and a half long. Everything else was medical mumbo jumbo. I just hoped the surgery would be the start of something positive, something tangible. Mama told me later that our family doctor said the surgery would (they hoped) help me to hold my head up in a wheelchair.

"Where are all the people?" I joked to the nurse who was hooking up my IV in the operating room.

"What?" she asked from under her mask.

"You know, the gallery…like on TV," I explained.

She thought the juice she was shooting into my veins was making me talk funny. She didn't reply. Just as well. Her face was looking wavy. *Why isn't she laughing at my joke, the sour…*

Then I checked into Motel Becalmed. That place where not even a dream is recalled.

Do you ever wonder what your subconscious is thinking and doing under anesthesia? I didn't have one of those out-of-body experiences, but I'd bet the hole out of a doughnut that I was dreaming. I never sleep without dreaming. God talks to me in dreams. Not always, but when he does, I know it. I'm not sure how to interpret all of them, but he definitely communicates to me through dreams. My favorites come as new songs. A song has to be saved immediately or it's lost. Some dreams come as messages and I call them night visions. You know the ones: they state their case, and then wake you so you can chew on it.

There was no blissful linger from a spiritual encounter when I awoke in the recovery room after surgery. It was more like awaking from a rendezvous in heaven just to discover you're in hell. I was strangling, and I couldn't tell the woman who kept saying, "Swallow, Sandra. Swallow." I needed desperately to go back to that painless, fearless state of unconsciousness. She was sucking debris from my throat, but it wasn't enough: a few tires, hubcaps, a couple of Volkswagens, and then a city bus before the lights began to fade, and I was sure I wouldn't return.

But not returning wasn't in the plan.

The surgery I'd hoped would deliver my miracle drained me of what strength I'd had. It hurt to swallow. To speak. Eating was unthinkable. Necessary medications choked me, so they were liquidized. The bitter potion burned like white lighting. I felt like I had a hen egg stuck in my throat. I lapsed back into the desire for sleep like a drunk craves wine. A prescribed stupor was better than reality. Let the world go on without me. I no longer cared.

Dr. Berkley interrupted my sleep to admire his good-looking scar on my neck on a regular basis. "It looks good, even if I did do it," he'd brag. Only a surgeon could relate to a comment like that. I can't say that Dr. Holm's knife to my hip was as tidy, but who would see it anyway? He kept his own watchful eye on its healing, though. But I couldn't see it…and I couldn't feel it. And I really didn't care.

The infamous Dr. Wingard seemed to be warming up now that I didn't give a rip either way. I never found out if he assisted Dr. Berkley during surgery. Probably not, because he never seemed too interested in the carving on my neck being unsightly. He watched it more with a cautious eye.

Mama resumed her regimen of sanitary upkeep. Daddy did everything but squirt my limbs with WD40. And my Jerry was never far from my side.

With all that attention and Mark 11:23 staring me in the face, how could I not return to civilization? I didn't yet realize it, but I was a survivor, a performer from birth, and the curtain was up. But the road to recovery is never without bumps. Just when the hen egg in my throat had shrunk to a wren's egg, an X-ray revealed the anterior portion of the bone graft to be out about one to two millimeters. Dr. Berkley braced himself for a scene. Grim faced, he said, "We've got to go back in."

"No! I can't go through that again," I cried. The memory of the strangling, debris sucking, and pain was too fresh. *Lord, anything but that. Let him say I'll never walk again. That I'm going to die. I don't have to believe him. But, please, don't make me go through that again. Not now, Lord, not that.*

"Can't we leave it alone? Does it absolutely have to be fixed?"

"In my best judgment, I think we should go in and reset it. It won't be nearly as bad this time," he promised.

Dr. Berkley was ready for the familiar tears that heated my face. "We can do it next week," he said, patting my arm gently.

I looked at Mark 11:23 through tear-filled eyes. I thought of Kip at home, needing his mama. It *was* the first promise Dr. Berkley had made me. I'd give him one more chance, but after that…

"Okay," I whispered.

The dread of another surgery preyed on my peace. I was beside myself with desperation. I'd been praying. Everybody had been praying. But now, I needed to get in God's face with something stronger than before. Not in an accusing way. In a way where he could see I meant to do business with him. The little red King James Bible the girls at work had given me for my birthday one year was on the nightstand. When we were alone, I asked Jerry to get it.

He, too, was at the point of desperation. "What do you want me to read?" he asked.

"Find Mark 11:23." It was on the card over my head, but I needed to hear it coming from his lips. I needed to know it was engraved on his heart also, because he was the other half of me.

He read it slowly, savoring each word, searching for a promise to hold like a seed in his hand. *For verily I say unto you, That whosoever shall say unto this mountain, Be thou removed, and be thou cast into the sea; and shall not doubt in his heart, but shall believe that those things which he saith shall come to pass; he shall have whatsoever he saith.*

Maybe it was because it was coming from the lips of the man I loved, but I believed it like I'd never believed it before. I didn't understand it. But I believed it.

Fighting back tears, I asked, "Jerry, will you pray with me?"

His eyes glazed over like a gray-blue lake, and with the seriousness of a father holding his baby for the first time, he gently laid the Bible on my chest, and then gathered my right hand into his. His words were simple, soft, and sincere. He asked for a miracle, and my prayer meshed with his in agreement, as it says in Matthew 18:19. We were one entity in two parts, but a third Spirit joined forces with us at that moment.

Hell itself cannot sever love's unseen cord. The word is *powerful, stronger than a two-edged sword*. Not every prayer we've prayed since then has manifested. The problem is never on God's end. He delights in giving us the desires of our hearts. He wants the word to work for us. Could God, who is love, ever say something he doesn't mean? Or could he change his mind? Never. But we are not always united in focus and expectation.

The second surgery was performed without difficulty. Dr. Berkley was right—it wasn't nearly as bad as the first time. Although I recovered speedily from the minor setback, the wandering chip of bone continued to meander. Dr. Berkley decided to leave it alone.

\* \* \*

I remember playing around the oil stove that stood in the corner of our living room when I was no older than three, and my parents warning me to stay away from it. I remember it because the three streaks of red flesh that whelped on my right arm when I didn't obey left a lasting impression. Crying would have given me away, so I gritted my teeth and concealed my pain. Of course, it wasn't long before my mom spotted the burn. My fear of a spanking melted when she held me tightly and salved my arm.

I remember sticking my finger in the white box in our refrigerator on the day I turned five. What came out was as sweet as icing, but when I asked Mama what was in the box, she said, "It's a chicken." I knew something was up. When Mama brushed my hair in the middle of the day, and the neighborhood kids started showing up with gifts, I figured out I was having a party. It's funny, the only gift I distinctly remember is a pair of green cotton socks. They were uglier than sin. Why do we retain what we disdain?

I remember tossing a coin in the wishing well at Linville Caverns the summer following the first grade. My wish was that Mama and Daddy would never find out that I didn't drink my milk at lunch the entire year. Fear of disapproval made a lasting impression. And how could I forget Grandpa Davis coming to school in his black Chevy pick-up when I was in the second grade? Mrs. Hilda had the gall to call and tell him I had chicken pox. *How could this be happening?* I thought. There I was decked out like a copper penny, proudly waiting for our first after-school "Brownie" meeting. I would have gladly given my ice cream money not to miss that meeting.

Mrs. Brendle was my all-time favorite teacher. Her youthful vitality made the fourth grade memorable. And that was the year Daddy bought me a pony that provided many memorable experiences to boot. Skipper was as rambunctious as a pup, but as stubborn as a mule. He always seemed to know when Daddy wasn't in sight. He'd buck and send me flying through the air, and then run like a wild maverick.

That was about the time that horses became a neighborhood fad. Daddy bought Mama a beautiful Appaloosa mare named Penny, but Mama was a cautious rider, to say the least. Not at all like me, who became princess of the rodeo when I saddled up. Daddy, who was no horse trainer, tried to break the colt I had won with a dollar raffle ticket at a horse show. The memory of Daddy's face when I told him I'd won a horse is an impression not likely to be unhitched from my mind's eye. We named my prize colt Diamond Jubilee because he was brown with a white spot on his rump, but Spot would have suited him better because when turned loose, he'd follow you like a dog.

The day of "the race" is a highlighted memory. My pony Skipper was feeling his oats on this particular Sunday afternoon neighborhood ride. He always wanted to be in front of the pack, like he had something to prove because he was just a pony. When Thad Speer challenged me to a race against his cutting horse to the end of the field and back, I agreed, and we lined up for the countdown. I could feel Skipper's blood rise—ready, set, go—and the chase was on. But as soon as I tightened my legs on Skipper's side, the reins meant nothing. He turned into a blaze of fire, short legs disappearing in the tall grass. When we neared the end of the field, the long-legged animal under Thad was at least two horse lengths ahead when, without warning, Skipper turned around on a dime and dashed toward the finish line where our spectators waited. My cheeks were pinned to my ears and my ponytail was keeping time. When Skipper reached the others, he stopped so abruptly that I did a summersault over his head. My loafers shot into the air like two skeet, and I landed hard on my back.

My parents nearly had simultaneous heart attacks, but nothing was broken except my pride as Skipper took off like a convict in a black and white suit. In spite of the fact that he's probably in hell today, the fun I had with that pony is still a fond memory.

When X-rays after the accident made my doctors ask if I'd had a previous neck injury, my parents recalled the racing fiasco. (An MRI twenty-six years later revealed that my second and third vertebra are fused together. "Probably born that way," the doctor said.)

My archive of memorable events—good and bad—has framed my life. I wasn't here for Pearl Harbor, but I guess everyone living on November 22, 1963, recalls where they were and what they were doing when they got the news that President Kennedy had been shot. I was in my freshman gym class when Principal Thomas Wooten made the intercom announcement. Everyone froze. Our generation had never experienced anything so savage. We read about such things in history books but could not contemplate living in that kind of society. Peace had been the agenda during Eisenhower's rein, and now this. Fear and disbelief grabbed our youthful hearts. And the brutal death of the president was televised for the world to see—over and over. It's baffling how the gruesome, heart wrenching, and devastating grind unforgettable pictures in one's mind.

Why doesn't my mind replay the high-school basketball games when our team won? I vaguely remember those nights when we were on top of the world. But I can still feel the ache in my gut from the night we blew up in the finals and gave Jonesville the win on a silver platter. I wanted to get in Coach Morgan's face and scream, "You forget how to cuss?"

Why is it that early memories can be so haunting? The cold slap in the face from an angry parent. The bitter gift of young love gone sour. Dreams of a beautiful church wedding and you flowing down the aisle as center attraction end up as just that: dreams. So you move on and dream of friends and family showering you with teeny-tiny baby clothes to hold and smell until the baby's grand arrival. But instead, you are the only fan of the life you're carrying, and you tremble at the thought of losing the heart that beats within you. You've failed at everything else, so why should you succeed at giving life to another?

Are they not all hollow dreams that melt like a Popsicle sliding down the stick on a sultry day? And you, you stand in the cold world like an unprepared solo.

And now life's ultimate betrayal: You're flat on your back with nothing but a head, and the violinist is mewling out a song.

*Yoo-hoo, memory taunter. Excuse me, but there's another stanza.*

\* \* \*

It was a Sunday night to remember. Visitors were gone, and the nurses had done their things: temp, bag, turn, record. Finally, it was just Jerry and me, and he seemed feisty. His eyes were unusually bright. Lit up by the deep blue shirt he was wearing, no doubt. The one with the laid back collar that he wore with the blue and pink plaid bell-bottoms. He chatted with more energy in his voice than usual. Kip said this. Kip did that. And then, out rolled the most preposterous request: "Why don't you try to move your big toe on your left foot?"

"What?"

"Try to move your big toe on your left foot."

"Uh, I can't see it," I replied, with a touch of smuggery. "And, I can't feel it, remember?"

But he bounced to the end of my sickbed with a one-legged leap and a silly grin. "Hey, you've got to start somewhere."

"Yeah, but…"

"I'll hold your foot up so you can see it, concentrate on that one big toe."

*Concentrate? This man is dead serious.* It wasn't normal for Jerry to be so assertive. I liked it. Wished I could do something about it. But I didn't have a clue as to how to reconnect my brain with the nerves that would tell that toe to move. But oh, how I wanted to give a stellar performance right now! I needed to for him, for both of us. The air was thick with anticipation. His belief in me was like adrenaline to my soul. *Oh God, if you've ever helped me, help me now.*

Reader, please enter my skin here: You're lying face up on a sterile hospital bed. You know you are, because you can see. You can hear. And you can feel—the clamps in your head, the water that periodically trickles down your cheeks, the knat that lights on your nose. You can feel—the heart that throbs for your child, the desire for your lover, the nearness of God within you. And you can think and speak.

You've been asked to perform, a miracle no less, by the one you want most at this moment to please—your soulmate, your sweetheart, your friend. How can you look into those eyes and deny him his request? He may never have this passion, this fire, again. So you reach deep with the hands of your soul into a place you've never before entered. Until now, you didn't even know it was there.

You close the eyes in your head, and open the eyes of your inner self. *Where, oh God, can I find life among this complex creation that the curse has dared to defile?* You're afraid to take your eyes off the coach at the end of the bed who has your foot in his hand like the "holder" on a windy day waiting for the kickoff. Anything less than a miracle will make him look like a fool.

A faint voice feathers a preposterous thought through your mind, "It's in your nose."

You almost snicker. *My nose?* The weak part of you wants to retreat, but there's no turning back now. It seems too weird for reasoning, but something that's dominating you says that it makes a smidgen of sense: You think of one thing (your toe), but move another (your nose). Crazy? Maybe. But what do you have to lose?

"Now! Do it now!" shouts the silent voice.

Before human reasoning has a chance to deter you, you simultaneously open the eyes in your head and wiggle the nose on your face. But you know the nose on your face is really the toe on your foot, held by the love of your life. And this, my precious confidant, ignites a flicker of movement of the toe in question. A flicker so ephemeral a bat of the eye would miss it. But the eyes you adore are filled with hope; he wouldn't have missed it for the world.

He jumps.

Your heart jumps.

"Can you do that again?" he asks.

But you don't know the answer; you didn't do it that time. Or did you? So you close your eyes, quickly before you lose momentum, and wiggle your nose—genie-like—again.

It moves again.

And again.

And you both know that more than a dead toe has resurrected on this monumental night—you've moved heaven, and nothing will ever be the same.

\* \* \*

The love in the room superseded romance, it was spiritual. The memories that used to taunt like plagues were being replaced by a memory more deserving of brain space. It was a moment I knew I'd have to share. I was still immobile. Still paralyzed. But by the grace of Almighty God, not as paralyzed as five minutes before. It might not have merited Carnegie Hall, but this tiny performance, this earthly impossibility, was all the evidence I needed that the Rock of Gibraltar was about to move—not by me, but by the Rock of Ages. God had answered our prayer for a miracle. I knew it. Jerry knew it. And all of hell couldn't stop it!

Jerry ran down the hall to the nursing station and returned with an audience. I repeated my moving-toe performance for anyone who would watch. This little pig went to market. This little pig stayed home. This little pig had roast beef. And this little pig cried, "Praise the Lord," all night long!

Jessie Myers, my dear, petite Florence Nightingale, who sat with me faithfully from midnight to 8:00 a.m., was to us like family. One look at the two of us, and she knew something was up. She and I celebrated the rest of the night.

The late hour didn't stop Jerry from beating on my parents' door with the good news before joining Kip at his sister's house. It was a night for the books, with the promise of a sequel. God said, "Here, my child," and I—we—took it with thanksgiving. And from that moment on I never once entertained the thought that I wouldn't walk again. Never once.

\* \* \*

Up until now, I'd had no warning when it was time to use the bathroom, but the previous night's performance boosted my confidence: I was on the bedpan when Dr. Wingard made his morning rounds.

"I'll catch her later," he told the nurse.

"Oh, no you won't," I spurted. With widened eyes, I said to the nurse, "Don't let him leave…get him back in here."

She caught him before he slipped away. "She has something to show you."

Knowing that Dr. Wingard's gifts in life didn't include patience, I got right to the point with him. "Take the sheet off my feet."

His brows rose, but he obeyed and lifted the sheet to my knees, as if unveiling a shrine. "Watch my left foot," I said. And the nose-wiggling, toe-moving attraction began.

"When did this happen?" he asked.

"Last night," I beamed.

"Do it again," he ordered, and I gave him my best performance.

He picked up the chart at the end of my bed and scribbled something on it. Kirt Orman said nothing. He didn't have to; his eyes always spoke for him. Dr. Wingard praised me like a teacher might praise a kindergartner who had colored within the lines for the first time. But that was my fault. I had a little-girl spirit, and people respond to us as we see ourselves. Dr. Wingard couldn't deny that moving my toe was progress, but he did not visualize it as a promise that I'd walk again. He left with a wink and an exultation to "keep up the good work."

When Jessie came in that night, she did the unthinkable and let me read what he had written on my chart: _Moved big toe on left foot! Very unusual!_

Miracles 101 is not among a medical student's criteria, so I understood Dr. Wingard's caution. But I knew God had visited us the night before. He may have sent my miracle via an angel. Or he may have reached his long arm of mercy right down to where we were. I didn't see Jesus in my room, but trees sway when the wind blows, and dogwoods bloom in spring, and we don't demand to see the wind or to touch the seasons. So why is it so hard to acknowledge that the creator of the universe might simply do something because he wants to? I've pondered many times why God didn't totally heal me instead of moving only one toe. There's a connection between what Jerry suggested and what took place that is a little deep for me to grasp. I'm convinced that God planted it in Jerry's mind to hold my foot up and have me concentrate—put a demand—on that area of my body. Could it be that in his infinite wisdom God chooses to move some mountains one pebble at a time?

# 7

## A TIME FOR EVERY PURPOSE

*…weeping may endure for a night, but joy cometh in the morning.*
—PSALMS 30:5

YOU HAVE TO BE CAREFUL when mountains begin to move, or you could just change valleys. This is especially true if those around you only see your present Gibraltar. I found myself wanting to hum that old Ray Charles tune, "It's Crying Time Again," when I'd think about how much digging remained in my tedious excavation. God was depositing nuggets to my heart's bank each day, and if I could trust his management of my portfolio through the rough times, I'd eventually cash in. But perseverance through hard times is like holding your breath under water—your lungs scream for air, but the vision of your goal holds you under.

I had loved ones, though, who had not yet seen with their own eyes the "new me." The me who could not sit up or reach out to give them a hug. As much as I wanted everyone near, my shoulders were saddled with the dread of their first-time reaction, and the duty that bound me to give them hope. So, not all my sobby tears were selfishly motivated—love hurts when others hurt, cries when they cry.

\*   \*   \*

Unlike my brother, I had children for parents—almost. Mama was eighteen and Daddy was nineteen. So that explains why my maternal grandparents shared an equal part, or more, in raising me, which in turn explains why Mama always said I acted like a "little old lady" until I started first grade at East Bend Elementary and was exposed to other children. Then, she says, I "went wild."

A child usually prefers that his or her mother stay at home, but Mama's job at Hanes Knitting Mill helped us to have the little extras, like store-bought clothes, and I don't regret the time I spent on my grandparents' farm. I was fortunate to have both sets of grandparents close at hand during childhood. To me, there is no better place to raise a child than on a farm. The land has more gut glue than asphalt cities; that's probably why so many country-raised adults return after awhile. If you ask most city kids where corn comes from, they'd most likely say the grocery store. But when you see it mature from a kernel to a stalk, and then harvested and preserved by your own flesh and blood, you don't know it at the time, but when it eventually swims in a bowl of cream on Sunday's dinner table…well, it becomes more than a meal—it's an event. Especially if you've got a plate of home-made biscuits to sop it up with, and I did a lot of sopping.

I never visited a zoo as a child but I interacted with enough animals, both wild and tame, to love and respect their natures. There was always a dog in my life, and each had its saga: The nameless puppy who froze in the outhouse. Scooter, who napped under Daddy's Jeep one time too many. Brownie, who I would have died for. And Tricksie, Brownie's replacement. If you got bit, it was usually by a neighborhood dog, and you didn't cut its head off and send it to Raleigh—you doused the bite with Mercurochrome and went about your business. Or so was the case with me.

Experiencing firsthand those who hammer out a living by the sweat of their brow with no guarantee that harvest will bring satisfactory reward doesn't necessarily make a kid more thankful for the small necessities in life. That comes later. And the land, rather than books, educated most people I knew who were my grandparents' age. They raised their children during the tough Depression, so they knew how to live with less and stretch a dollar. That alone demanded respect. Mama recounts the days when her breaking a fruit jar would bring tears to Grandma Davis' eyes. Those days were over, but the simplicity of my grandparents' lifestyles was instilled. This generation is sometimes considered simple-minded, but their educations were gleaned through experience instead of in the classroom.

I rarely saw my grandparents incorporate very much recreation into their lives, certainly not as we do today. Work and worship were their priorities, but they had their moments. Just thinking about my daddy's father, Grandpa Hobson, down on all fours crawling toward me like a jolly bear, his laugh forming perfectly round circles at the cliff of each cheek, still sends a surge through my body. He had a rotund belly and a gold tooth that glowed when a smile separated his lips; he would have made a great Santa. And although I knew the next act would be Granny Hobson entering the room with a silk stocking over her head, a squeal would erupt in spite of me. She was absolutely the spookiest thing I'd ever seen with her nose mashed flat and her eyes squinted shut.

In the winter, their rented farmhouse seemed cave-like, cold and dark. Except for the room where they stayed and slept. One could roast marshmallows from the penetrating heat that emanated from the black potbelly stove kept chock-full of wood. Like most houses built before or during the Depression, the house was poorly insulated, so they only fed the stoves in the rooms that necessitated heat and kept the other rooms closed off. The sun and Grandma's wood stove kept the kitchen toasty. But she was the center attraction. I can still hear her voice rise and fall as she hollered, "Let's e—eat," in a high-pitched tone. She's the only "Annis" I've known, but the name fit her strawberry-red hair and freckles well. Even though Grandpa growled at her a lot, he was her knight in shining armor till the end.

They eventually bought a small farm where they lived out their retirement years, but my memory likes to drift back to that living room where the his-and-her chairs sat on each side of the woodstove, and all who entered knew they were assigned to Annis and Leo. The couch pushed the front window curtain tight against the wall, and an iron bed with a yellow spread served two purposes: sitting and sleeping. Next to the bed, the black and white Zenith's wires ran out the west window. And the words *Only one life, it will soon be passed, only what's done for Christ will last* pulsates from the grape-colored plaque on the dingy plank wall like an eleventh commandment.

More than a few times, I caught Grandpa pinching Granny in a questionable place. She would always holler, "Lee-o!" in a disapproving tone, and he'd laugh that unmistakable laugh of his.

But never did I catch Grandpa Davis doing such a thing, and I was with my maternal grandparents enough to know should a thing like that happen. Occasionally, Grandpa Davis would cut loose and dance a jig on the kitchen floor when he felt good. People back then didn't need music if they took a notion to dance. I can't recall Grandma Davis initiating playfulness; she was usually busy at something, or else she was taking a siesta in her red rocking chair around two in the afternoon on weekdays when "The Art Linkletter Show" came on. But she employed a silent laugh that shook her whole body at the antics of the rest of us.

During the summer months, I'd often follow Grandpa Davis to the barn to feed the cows, pigs, chickens, and his workhorse, Charlie. I can still smell the rich, black barnyard dirt that Grandma used to dig up to put around her flowers. "The blacker, the better," she'd say. When you reach my age the sounds and smells from your childhood are sometimes more vivid that yesterday's pot-roast. The memory of the fragrance from a deep-purple, sunny-yellow, and snow-white iris, along with her famous "bubby bush," still tickles my senses. A dark maroon, spidery bud from her bush tucked in a handkerchief was perfume for Sunday-go-to-meeting time. I can still feel the cool latch on the tattered barn door and smell the blend of metal and rust. I hear it click as it falls, then swings, allowing the door to squeak open. The weathered-gray barn was the first of many essential farm buildings you approached as you wound down the long dirt drive leading to their three-room house.

Grandpa would toss hay down from the loft—a place forbidden to me—then pitch a bale into each stall and spread some on the ground behind the barn. I thought he was being ornery not to let me climb into the loft, but now that I'm a grandparent, I understand his over-protective nature. And losing his oldest son, Donald, who was in flight training during the war in 1942, had to tighten his grip on the rest of us. I can vaguely remember Grandpa taking care of Uncle Donald's sickly dog, Bingo, and the day he drug him off by his chain to his final resting place.

It amazed me how Grandpa would reach high above his head and stick his hand under a fat-feathered hen to retrieve eggs from a nest. I had no problem being near a meandering cow chewing her food the second time or reaching up to give Charlie a rub, but for some reason I was afraid of anything with the ability to peck. I'd had enough encounters with a ruffled hen protecting her chicks! But watching Grandpa's bravery as he reached into the unprotected darkness was almost like being brave myself. I could only imagine one thing worse than being pecked: a black snake coiled up in one of those nests.

I can still hear him chanting, "C'mon, c'mon," in the evening when he wanted to lure the cows from their grassy haven to the barn so he could feed them hay. No matter where they were hiding, under the shade of a tall oak or near a water hole, they'd line up like school kids and head toward his voice. I used to mimic his chant in an effort to call them up, but they recognized the voice of an impostor and knew they'd get no hay from me.

Before I started to school, Daddy would take me to Grandpa and Grandma Davis' house at bedtime so they wouldn't have to get me up so early. In the summer, I'd ask Grandpa to wake me when he got up so I could go with him for the early-morning feeding. "Now Snooky," he'd say, "there ain't no use of you git'n up that early." And most of the time when the sun had just begun to light the day, I'd agree. I am to this day what they call a "night person," inherited from Grandma's side of the family, I've been told. But occasionally, I'd be up by the time he'd return with a bucket of freshly squeezed milk and some eggs still warm from laying. Grandma would place a sterile, white cloth over the milk bucket and skim the cream off, which she used to make butter in her wooden churn.

I'd be at his heels when Grandpa would hook the plow up to Charlie and gee-haw him through the garden or some other piece of land that needed turning. I've listened with a sad heart many times as he reminisced over his rough childhood and how he was made to walk behind a mule with the reins around his neck and keep a plow in the rows while sporting a broken collarbone. His mother died when he was three, and his wish of locating her grave was not to be, despite walking through the graveyard at Prospect United Methodist Church many times hoping to find it. There were just too many unmarked graves for him to remember that far back.

Occasionally, I'd go with him up town to T.D. Smitherman's store in his black Chevy truck. In addition to the usual staples, he'd buy Hershey's Chocolate Bars and ice-cream on a stick, and Pauline Old-ham (T.D. Smitherman's daughter) would insist I choose a piece of candy (without charge) from her glass counter, like she did every other kid who came in. You had to walk into a refrigerated room to get your milk and up a wooden-floor ramp to find school supplies and paper products. She'd pump your gas if you needed her to, and she would write the amount of the purchases in a spiral notebook for those who couldn't pay.

Many nights through the years when sleep has failed me, I've retraced my childhood memory of the way the farm was back then. The apple tree near the barn that I climbed and Grandpa had to retrieve me from. The roots extending like giant legs from the mighty oak by the tobacco barn. The mud hole I'd jump across after a generous rain. The wild strawberry patch where Grandma could be found each day that they were producing—and oh, her scrumptious pies! The cucumber patch that grew like a thicket before it yielded white cucumbers from her special seeds—she sold pickles for twenty-five cents a jar to strangers, but she'd never charge someone she knew. The earthy smell of the dirt floor in the pump house. The dusty cellar where they hand-tied tobacco after it cured. The blackness inside the smokehouse that was once used to cure hams. The clean smell of an afternoon shower of rain and its hypnotizing effect from a front-porch rocker. And grass, lots of it, apple green and spidery.

Grandpa possessed a respect for a storm that has been lost with time. At the first sound of thunder, you found a quiet place and stayed there. I can see him now on the porch whittling on a stick, saying little as the stick shrunk and the rain waned. I used to enjoy hanging my head off the porch and letting the falling water wet my hair, so I received more than a few scoldings for being too active during a summer storm. He may have exaggerated his point, but I carry a healthy respect for thunder and lightning to this day.

If given a choice, I would've stayed at home where my guardians were younger and our house was more fashionable. But looking back, I'm thankful I was with blood-kin who loved me. To have missed Grandma's fried chicken and gravy on a regular basis would have been unfortunate. To have been absent for her pumpkin, strawberry, and sugar pies (sometimes doused with cocoa) would have been unbearable—and Mama hadn't yet mastered the art of cookery. "Beep," as Grandma came to be known, expressed her love through cooking. At the aroma of a plain yellow cake rising in her oven, my dash to the kitchen always found a little batter spooned out on a piece of waxed paper. Grandpa disliked icing, but I was so happy for my little pone that it didn't make a cat's whiskers difference to me that it wasn't iced.

Sights, sounds, smells, tastes, and textures fill memory's window when I need to lapse into a time when the world's pace better fits my present-day gait. Daddy glistened with flecks of aluminum foil and smelled like tobacco. Mama felt soft like foam and smelled like Elizabeth Arden. Grandma sounded of work and smelled like baking bread. Grandpa smelled like bark and looked rich with contentment in his bibbed overalls and gray-brimmed felt hat.

When he retired from farming in 1963, Grandpa also retired his bibs, replacing them with casual pants. It was an upgrade for them when they bought our little white-shingled house with two bedrooms and a bath, and we moved into our new house next door. But nothing was the same after that. I didn't miss the farm until later, but when it hit me, I knew an important era was forever gone. But what can dampen the senses captured and preserved in memory? How grave the need to cultivate the senses of the young!

\* \* \*

Grandma Davis had visited the hospital after the accident several times before Grandpa mustered the nerve to come. He had his gray-brimmed hat in hand the day Mama brought him to my room. He stepped quietly to my bedside to evaluate the situation for himself. I sensed his uneasiness, his shock, as his faded-blue eyes scanned the gadgets attached to me. It all looked so foreign to him. The sense of helplessness that engulfed the one whose nature was to caution and protect, forced him to walk away without comment.

"Where'd you go, Grandpa?" I asked. But Mama covered her lips with a finger, and I understood his need to recoil—he didn't want me to see him cry. Mama and I picked up the conversation and moments later he emerged. But oh, how I wanted to arise and say, "Look Grandpa, I'm all better! You don't have to worry anymore!" This was the man whose footprints I'd followed through the red clay for the better part of the first decade of my life. The one who, even though I was grown and making my on way, thought it necessary to slip me a five spot when he sensed a need. So I swallowed the lump in my throat and asked, "How's your cat doing, Grandpa?"

My heart still stings when I'm forced to recall Grandpa's first hospital visit. But behind closed eyes, I see him leaned back on the back legs of a slated porch chair, whittling nothing out of a stick as the rain falls on the old tin roof and the thunder claps in a dark distant sky, and I dare to stretch my head into God's domain.

\* \* \*

Mark was a strong-willed child, but he had a soft spot that only those closest to him knew about. He made the comment once that everything was going good until I brought Kip home when he was only three and a half. The two of them displayed as much sibling rivalry as any two brothers, and were as different as night and day. Our age difference made me seem more like a second mother than a sister to Mark. That changed when he grew up, of course.

Kindergarten wasn't mandatory when my brother turned five, and because Mama quit work after he was born, he had never been away from home. She wanted to enroll him in a kindergarten program to prepare him for first grade. Thinking I had the perfect solution, we enrolled Mark in kindergarten and Kip in daycare at the same facility in Winston-Salem. I didn't go to work until ten-thirty in the morning and planned to drop the two of them off and Daddy would pick them up in the afternoon. So much for bright ideas! Mark nearly pulled my clothes off my body when I started to leave. I can still hear him screaming: "Don't leave me here, Sandra. Don't leave me here!"

It was not a good feeling.

Desperate to calm him, I retorted without thinking, "Mark, if you don't stop crying the teacher might spank you!" No sooner than the words left my mouth, I sensed I'd dug my own grave. Mrs. Sample's lips tightened, and she curtly escorted me into another room. When she was finished, I, too, was in tears. Humiliated and forlorn, I pulled myself from Mark's clutches and scurried to my car.

My second mistake was looking back: Two-year-old Kip had his face pressed against the playground fence in an effort to see me, and another kid came up and bopped him right on the head. Need I tell you my day was shot? I pulled Kip out after the second day and reported to my parents that if they wanted their son to go to kindergarten, they'd have to take him. Mark, the little squirt, never pulled that with Daddy, who ended up taking him to kindergarten on his way to work. And had I been mature enough to give it a little time, Kip would have adjusted, also. Mark ended up being Mrs. Samples pick for master of ceremonies at graduation, and rightly so—he was clearly her pet all year. Unfortunately, the chicken pox picked that week to dot him with blisters, preventing him from attending.

Mark was free to come in and out our trailer as if he lived there. As a matter of fact, I kept him while my parents were away the Saturday that I went into early labor with Kip, lifting him back and forth over the ditch Jerry had hued out to underpin our trailer. I drug Mark with me through the path in the woods to tell Grandma that I was spotting with five more weeks to go, then drug him back when she told me I'd best get home, because I'd probably deliver soon. I was shaking inside like a deserted kitten—my doctor hadn't got around to telling me what delivery would be like, Mama struggled to say the word "pregnant" in my presence, and if there were explanatory books, I didn't know where to find them. I didn't share the threat of early delivery with another soul, but Mark and I went to the basement at my parents' house and washed all of his old cloth diapers, just in case. I'd just seen Dr. Petty the previous week, and according to him, I had another five weeks to term. But ready or not, nature took its course and Kip was born—small, but healthy—the next morning.

Mark was an inquisitive kid. The first winter Jerry and I were married our not-yet-sown-yard was muddy from a downpour, and we heard Mark calling us from outside. We flung open the door and found him standing ankle deep in mud hollering, "I'm stuck, Jerry. I'm stuck!" Before he rescued him, Jerry took his picture, which irritated Mark even more. He looked like a porcelain Precious Moment's kid standing there frozen in mud and looking innocently grim.

I'm persuaded Mark was a gift dropped down from heaven to keep my parents young. If I hadn't been with Daddy when we took Mama to the hospital, I don't think he could have got her admitted. My junior English class was already in session when I got to school that day. "Well, what is it?" Mr. Barnes asked, when I sneaked into class.

"A black-headed boy," I replied, grinning from ear to ear. And I liked him a whole lot better than the monkey I'd begged for.

\* \* \*

Kip filled Jerry's arms like a good-will parcel as they entered my room that Sunday afternoon. He was dressed in the navy and white plaid pants, red shirt, and navy sport coat Mama bought for him to wear to his school's fall festival. His hair fell like corn silk around his collar, illuminating my room with the brightness of his presence. His blue eyes were curious with wonder at the strangeness of the room. He had only a mental picture of what to expect from the descriptions

Jerry had given him as preparation for this day. Jerry leaned Kip over me and I felt his tender, cool lips touch my cheek. "Hey, Mama," he said, before squirming from Jerry's arms and informing us that my room didn't look like his. (He remembered having a hernia repaired at age three, and referred to his scar respectfully as his "operator.")

Mama and Daddy eased Mark in at this point. Unlike Kip, the balloons and trinkets adorning my room did not fascinate him. Mark marched up to the right side of my bed, his eyes seesawing from the tongs to mine, and there he remained for the duration of his visit. Daddy showed him how to exercise my arm, and like a little trooper he took my right hand and began silently pumping my arm. As long as I'm blessed with the gift of memory, nothing will dampen the picture I cherish of those eyes as dark as chocolate drops glued to me, the hurt that glazed them, and the silent words my nine-year-old brother mouthed: I love you.

∗　∗　∗

From early on, Kip tried to hide emotion. He was around four, not over five, when he burst into the trailer one Saturday, BB gun in hand, and with a quivering chin proclaimed, "There's something wrong with that woodpecker out there!"

"You didn't shoot it, did you, Kip?" I asked.

"Well, I shot at it, but I know I didn't hit it," was his reply. And yes, he was quite young for a BB gun, but you had to know Kip and his daddy. Jerry was not slack in instilling safety and skill with weapons and their use in the sport of hunting from day one. I've often said that Kip was born with a gun in his hand, and that's not stretching it far. Hunting was Jerry's thing, and Kip inherited the love for it. You carry them for nine months inside your body—in my case eight—throw up regularly, stretch your skin beyond repair, endure the cross of contractions (without epidural), and the male child comes out a duplicate of the one that caused it all in the first place. But for some reason known only to God, you love them anyway. Kip's quivering chin was proof that a "good talking to" was lesson enough, for that day at least.

He was about nine or ten when he strung a piece of twine between two trees, attached a fishhook to the middle of it, and then baited it with sardines. Lucky for him, the poor cat survived. I pretty much threw up my hands after that.

But during his preschool years, Kip's dry eyes and quivering chin ruined many a day for me when I had to leave him with various babysitters. He did well in kindergarten; his teacher, Miss Minton, and I were best friends in school. But I can still see where I left him sitting with chin quivering the day I took him to meet his first grade teacher. Mrs. Tanner was African American, and he had minimal exposure to people of other races. It didn't take long, though, for him to warm to her, and I'm convinced Mrs. Tanner was influential in his handling my absence so well, as the accident happened early that school year. She had a big heart and went the extra mile. Kip soon forgot about her skin being different from his. It was Mrs. Tanner who Kip told, "If people will pray for my mama, she'll get better." Mrs. Tanner turned out to be a godsend, in addition to being a very good teacher.

I knew my baby boy was being well cared for. But who can know her child like a mother? He was with me before he was with any other. Nobody knew the signs of fear behind his timid smile like I, or the difference between him stretching the truth to tell a good tale and when you needed to take him bone serious. Nobody else knew the "Granny" story that I made up for Mark and him. Who else would know that reading him the story of Jesus calming the storm would calm his fears when the clouds turned dark and the winds began to blow?

After a long Sunday afternoon visit at the hospital, Mark left feeling he could help in the process of my getting stronger. I was the same big sister on the inside whose arms would always be open for him even though, at present, I could not lift them.

Kip stayed with Jerry and me until Jessie arrived late that night. Curled up in the recliner asleep, Jessie admired our offspring, smiled tenderly, and commented, "He looks just as I thought he would."

Healing tears rained on my pillow that night. I'd crossed another milestone, and the vision of the little soldier pumping my arm and the bundle that Jerry carried away was enough to keep me in the ring for one more round. Yielding to my contender, this thing that had me pinned to the bed, would never be a choice. There was way too much at stake.

\* \* \*

Weeping is a release valve for tension. I did my share of weeping during those days of transition, and I'll admit that after all these years, resurrecting memories has dimmed the vision of my monitor screen a few times. According to Hebrews 4:15, we have a high priest (Jesus) who is *touched by the least of our infirmities,* and was *in all points tempted as we are, yet without sin.* The fact that God feels what I, and every member of the human race feels, is a little heavy for me to grasp, but by faith I believe it. He is compassionate beyond our ability to comprehend the word. And by faith I can see with the dim eye of one who's limited by an earth suit, a morning bright and fair when *God shall wipe away all tears from their eyes; and there shall be no more death, neither sorrow, nor crying, neither shall there be any more pain: for the former things are passed away* as Rev. 21:4 proclaims.

God can feel what I feel, but I can't fathom what he must have felt when Jesus was so brutally beaten that he bore no resemblance to a man. I can't imagine what God felt when they spit in his son's face, thrust a crown of thorns into his precious head, and then drove rusty nails into his hands and feet. I've never known the kind of love that would permit that for a world of hell-bound sinners. But I am moved to tears that he did that for me. To think that his resurrected son is with him in heaven, preparing for us a place more glorious than tongue can describe, should bring us tears of joy. But sometimes I think we are so territorially blessed with the gospel message that we have become deadened to the dimension of that reality.

My grandparents left one by one: Grandpa Davis, then Grandpa Hobson, Grandma Davis, and lastly, Grandma Hobson. I believe by their lives and the word of their testimony that they're all in heaven. And if I could talk to them, I would tell them to save me a seat at the table, because I don't think it will be long before the trumpet blows.

I can imagine Granny Hobson hollering in a heavenly cord, "Let's e—eat!" as we all gather around the table for the Marriage Supper. Thinking about it makes me want to look yonder beyond the rolling, white clouds and chant (like only Grandpa Davis could), "C'mon, Lord Jesus. C'mon!"

# 8

## A TIME TO LEARN

*Let your conversation be without covetousness; and be content with such things as ye have: for he hath said, I will never leave thee, nor forsake thee.* —HEBREWS 13:5

THE MONTH OF OCTOBER was consumed with mere survival, and progress dallied with my emotions. If the earth's rotation dared to call light a new day, I needed to see a change in the status quo: the awakening of a new muscle, reign of a bodily function, a glint of finger movement, a touch felt. Anything. Yesterday's homage to progress made was a stale memory. Fueling my spirit with what had been accomplished, rather than what remained as dormant as a hibernating cub, was not easy. I could move my toes, feet, and legs minutely, but the effort was sapping. Upper body movement was even harder. I had managed some slight finger movement, but actual use of my hands was a seemingly unattainable mountain. I could push my arms off my chest when someone placed them there, but my hands remained wherever they were laid, or in some cases, dropped. A friend raised my right arm once to sponge me off and forgot and turned my hand loose in midair—I smacked myself in the face. Not wanting her to feel bad, I forced a smile when she laughed, but inside I was humiliated to despair. To feel my hand on my face without feeling my face on my hand lacked humor from where I lay.

Added to the obvious leach that zapped me of strength on a daily basis was my self-inflicted need to solve everybody else's problems. If I could have bottled my emotions like paint in a jar, I might have invented the crackle effect before its time. I thought God had placed me there to do maintenance on everybody else's lives. But the truth was, I'd had more change dumped on me than I could handle—anymore and I'd suffocate. Friends and family tried to keep my room deplete of news that might upset me, but eventually things seeped in. A few months before the accident, I got it in my head that I wanted a horse. I missed the riding I had done as a kid. Jerry wasn't fond of horses but didn't have a problem with me getting one, as long as I cared for it. Thad Speer, the neighbor I had the infamous race with as as a youngster, said he would pasture a horse, and pony for Kip, if I found what I was looking for. A couple that we were long-time friends with also liked to ride, and they wanted me to try a quarter horse they knew was for sale. So the three of us saddled up on a Sunday afternoon a couple of weeks before the accident and rode a long trail up Pilot Mountain. We crossed the Yadkin River several times before the assent through some pretty rough terrain. The horse rode hard, and I felt that saddle between my legs for a week like one feels a hat on your head after it's been removed. Spending a Sunday afternoon riding with old friends was exhilarating, and I figured I'd get back into shape after I got my own horse, which wouldn't be that one. When Jerry finally told me the couple had split, I fell apart like a two-dollar suitcase.

It was a well-known fact that a relative, with a heart as big as Texas, had a drinking problem. It was not unusual for him to show up in my room every few days, so if he missed a week, I suspected the worse and worried like I was his mother, even though he was older than my parents. I have learned that if you're bent toward being depressed, you'll succeed, and I didn't have to look far: Mama had a cold once and I asked a nurse to dial our family doctor so I could inform him; Daddy was admitted to the hospital with a kidney stone and I nearly had a breakdown; an elderly woman from our community died and I cried like a baby. The list goes on. If anyone ever needed an antidepressant it was I, but Valium was the closest thing to one that I was offered. Admitting depression would have created its own malady; I would've worried that I was relying on a pill to keep me from being depressed instead of trusting God.

Praying for others is one thing, but controlling change is like stopping a falling star. Maybe I thought being matchmaker, counselor, and repairer of anything broken was something productive I could still do from my position; but it was a poorly founded defense mechanism for my inability to repair my own brokenness. I had yet to learn to divide spirit, soul, and body. To me, spirit and soul were synonymous, and I let the soulish realm—my feelings and intellect—dominate most of the time. I could not keep my physical self unchanged, so I worked at keeping significant others from changing. It was, of course, a futile effort. Being Spirit led means drawing from the fruit placed in you through Christ's righteousness: love, joy, peace, longsuffering, gentleness, goodness, faith, meekness, and temperance. None of these nine naturally composes my flesh, and they are, at the most, superficial when attempted from my soul. Real fruit, fruit that will remain, comes by faith and not of ourselves, or else we'd boast. Learning to approach situations through prayer and faith in Jesus' name is the best way to move someone else's mountain. Still, the will of the other person plays a factor in the outcome.

Even though it wasn't happening fast enough for me, my attitude remained positive in regard to my moving limbs and expectations. The pragmatic Dr. Wingard viewed my expectation of returning to normal as false hope. I had already progressed far beyond what was medically logical because I was moving my lower extremities, but I was miles from being normal. The goal was to be able to sit up in a wheelchair before I could be moved to the rehabilitation center, and I couldn't even sit up in the bed yet. None of my present performances was impressive enough for him to view me as a potentially mobile person. Letting me down easy was not easy for him, but he did the best he could.

"You're expecting a miracle," he offered grimly, "but miracles only happen in places like Palestine."

Whoa! You'd have to be an ostrich to miss the implications in that comment. But he caught me off guard. If I replied, "Oh, you'll see, Mr. Skeptic," like I was thinking, I might eat my words. But if I allowed my spirit to come into agreement with his statement, it would have been like holding up a white flag to the enemy. So I said nothing, gritted my teeth, and set out to prove that the God of Abraham was also my God, and I, by means of "blood-bought" adoption, had been placed under the Abrahamic covenant of blessing just as if Jewish blood flowed literally through my veins. I did denote a hint of compassion in the doctor's voice, so I dared not ruin the chance of becoming his friend with fruitless argumentation—mark one up for me. I had made a point of trying really hard not to let him see the tears that seemed to irritate him. I did, however, record his statement of miracles only happening in places like Palestine in my archive of mental references, if for no other reason than to spur me on days when I was too weary to strain to find another active muscle. It's amazing what you can do when you're ticked!

*Hope deferred maketh the heart sick, but when the desire cometh, it is a tree of life* (Proverbs 13:12).

I've heard many good sermons, especially in the last decade, and have agreed with many revelations given to men and women of God. But it is not until God speaks a thing directly to me through my own set of circumstances that I can thoroughly walk in it. God gave me my Palestine experience when he visited my room that Sunday night and divinely thumped my toe. No sermon on the healing power of God could have embedded the kind of assurance in me that resulted from that experience. It took a One-on-one encounter, and it wouldn't have mattered if every doctor in the world had paraded through my room with their own argument of proof that I had not received a "miracle" and should not expect more. I expected more. Nothing could defer my hope or sicken my heart to the point of believing otherwise. Even though I was impatient, as far as I was concerned, it was a done deal. And right here in the good ole USA!

Andrew Wommack, a Bible teacher from Colorado, says that you cannot see in the natural what you have not seen already in your imagination. I know with certainty that I have lived out things that I have allowed myself to ponder to the point of envisioning; not all of them have panned out for the positive. That's why the God-given gift of imagination should be carefully guarded. Satan can roll a mini-series in our minds that will look appealing, but when acted out, it's like the kiss of death. Seeing myself walking again was a good mental image, and one I would not allow to be expunged. It was deeper than determination. The Holy Spirit was the photographer, and I was in the picture. Standing tall.

\* \* \*

The clement Dr. Berkley's comment the day before my transfer to John C. Whitaker Rehabilitation Center was also stout enough to retain: "The picnic's over."

I couldn't exactly relate five weeks in traction and two surgeries to a picnic. I knew a lot of hard work lay ahead, but I thought he was underestimating the fight-to-the-finish grit *I thought* I had. I was sure I was ready to advance, but it was becoming apparent that my goal and the goal set for me by the hospital staff were not the same. Someone from our state's vocational rehabilitation department had visited me with talk of "building ramps and lowering cabinets" in our home. The Lord knew what he was doing when he gave me a strong constitution; my boldness in counteracting the man's suggestions likely came across to him as denial, but my ears closed automatically at any hint of remaining in my present state.

My response to the (well-meaning) voice of others through the years has likely been interpreted as rudeness, or at the least, stubbornness. But the life behind my vision was, and still is, at stake. What if the woman with the issue of blood in Matthew 9:20 had listened to her scorners and failed to *stubbornly* press through the crowd? Positive change doesn't materialize by cowling or compromising for the sake of acceptance. Sometimes response can be letting negative statements roll off you like water on the proverbial duck's back; and that's not as simple as it may sound. Others demand counteraction. You may not win a congeniality contest, but when you're fighting for your life, you can't afford to be underdressed when damaging words come shooting toward you like bullets. Words may not break your bones, but when allowed, they can penetrate the most vital part of your existence: the human spirit.

"Are you ready for this?" Dr. Wingard asked the following morning when Jerry came to transfer me to my new residence. My affirmative response meant I was ready to go to the next level of healing, but he knew I could not calculate the cost at this point. It's not hard to get into the ring, but going all the rounds is another story. The tongs were gone for good, and the brace—a constant cross—was a reminder that pain comes before gain.

My legs dangled off the side of the bed like a Raggedy Ann doll when Dr. Wingard sat me up. He held a tight hand on my shoulder, and when our eyes met and he smiled, I felt I was moving away from a newfound friend. He knew I had not bought his Palestine comment. And he knew that all his training and expertise could not silence the voice that drives some people, that drove me.

Jerry swept all ninety-two pounds of me into his arms, and I was suddenly lost in a wheelchair made for Goliath. My attending nurse approached me with a black belt. "I need to strap you in with this," she stated.

"What for?"

"We fasten these around patient's stomachs when they're being transferred," she explained. "It helps to keep you from turning sick."

"Nah, I won't need it," I said. She looked up at the handsome doctor, but he just shrugged his shoulders and grinned, so she tossed the belt onto the empty bed.

"You work hard now," were his last words before Jerry pushed me away from my "safe place," the place where I'd been monitored by family and staff since my arrival.

Brightly painted walls and artwork decorated the halls that were heavy with traffic. I felt like I'd just squeezed out of a cocoon. As we moved along, the air touched my face with more vigilance than I'd felt in the five weeks I spent in my room. We said goodbye to the nurses that looked different somehow from this angle, the elevator dinged, and people stepped back to let us enter the next stage of challenges.

*They're staring at me. My legs. My hands drawn into bony fists. My greasy, two-scarred head. They're wondering what happened. They can't see my miracle.* I wanted to pull the stops and say, "Hey, nobody gets off until you watch me move something!" Pride always has something to prove. Poor me, I had no idea that they could have cared less.

I was relieved when the door finally opened and we were released to enter the ground floor. But like a bug in a jar the memory of two years back, when Jerry pushed me—empty-handed—out of this same hospital, taunted me. Recollection of a miscarriage, and probably our last chance for another child, sent a knife through my heart. I let my thoughts speak. "I wish we were leaving with a new baby."

"Me too," Jerry said. And then the bittersweet silence of the future verses the past ping-ponged in our brains until we reached the next door—the exodus from constant care to the wilderness where I would discover a new word for survival. A place where there was no time for petty quirks and peculiarities. Everyone was on equal ground at John C. Whitaker Rehabilitation Center. I'd need a new kind of grace if I made the journey to my Promised Land.

\* \* \*

When the elevator door opened on third-floor Whitaker, a lanky, dark-haired, thirty-something head nurse greeted us promptly. "You must be Sandra," she said, approaching us with a straight-lipped smile. "I'm Mrs. Allen."

Jerry gave his name and held out a hand. Knowing that I could not turn my head for the brace, she stopped in front of me. "You don't have a belt on," she observed.

"I made it fine," I said, wondering what magical powers that black belt I'd refused held. Mrs. Allen retrieved a clipboard from the nursing station facing the elevator.

"I think your mom is waiting in your room," she informed us, and then led us to the last room at the end of the hall.

Third-floor Whitaker sounded like a dormitory: TVs blasting from four-bed wards, patients conversing and laughing like roommates. A teenage boy with a yellow ponytail did a wheelie as he sped past us. "Hey Deb, I need you," he shouted.

"Just hold on, Skip. You're not the only patient on this floor, you know," a nurse carrying a Styrofoam pitcher retorted, as she whipped by. My insides tightened. *Will I be able to squelch this noise even in a private room?*

Mama had preceded us with plants, cards, and other memorabilia from the hospital. She rose from her chair, as if she needed to give the head nurse attention when we entered. Mrs. Allen gave the grand tour: a wardrobe for my clothes, a sink beside the suspending TV, and a bathroom equipped with an inviting shower you could roll a wheelchair into. The window on the right side of my bed overlooked the back parking area. Mrs. Allen flung the wardrobe open. "Our patients wear street clothes: jeans, warm-up suits, anything comfortable for therapy," she said. "Regular clothes will make you feel more at home."

I hated to tell her, but my home was thirty miles and thirty minutes down the road—I had no intention of getting cozy.

"The sooner you can dress yourself, the better," she added.

*Did she say, dress myself? My hands are two puppets attached to the ends of my arms, which by the way have no lifting gear, and my fingers are hooks.*

Why did I get the feeling I was about to pull hard time? At least at the hospital they had enough sense to notice I couldn't actually do anything. I mean, sure, I'd dress myself eventually when everything returns, but what did she expect me to dress myself with, my teeth? *And what's this stupid-looking, cherry-red ball hanging over the head of my bed—a rattler?*

My attitude was transparent, much to Mama and Jerry's embarrassment, and a volcano was about to erupt. Mrs. Allen noticed me eye-balling the object. "Oh yes," she explained, "this is how you can ring the nursing station if you need anything?"

*You mean, like food and water?*

The nurse smacked the swinging ball and a crackling voice responded, "Yes?"

"Just testing," Mrs. Allen spoke into the air. "Pretty neat, huh?"

*Oh yeah, here's the ball, now where's the chain?* I faked a smile.

"All you have to do is touch it with your head." She gave it another whack. Nothing.

Again.

"Yes?"

"It's just me."

"Okay."

We had been told that even family members would have to adhere to visiting hours at Whitaker. Jerry was planning to return to work, anyway, and physical therapy would take up most of my days, but I assumed Jessie would get to stay with me at night until I could make it on my own. When Mrs. Allen told me that would not be allowed, heat wormed up the back of my neck, and I exploded. "But I can't lift a finger!"

She squatted down in front of my chair on wheels like a teacher would to condescend to a child. "Well we're going to work on that," she said. "Tell you what, your nurse can stay tonight. How's that?"

It was time to let go. I knew it. But I was scared. More scared than I could ever remember. Being alone with nothing but a ball dangling conspicuously over my head like a hypnosis watch, and not knowing when I'd be able to manipulate it was overwhelming enough—I could scream if necessary—but that wasn't the real issue. The real issue was the emptiness of a room void of love—the stream of love that those closest to me had kept flowing. But they had lives outside the walls that centered around me—lives that needed to commence again, if only in part.

Mrs. Allen left the three of us to adjust to my new surroundings.

"At least Jessie can come and stay tonight," Mama stated. I bit my lip. "Yeah, that's good." But I couldn't tame the tears that washed my face.

"You'll be alright," Mama attemped to convince me. Mama's always been a stickler for keeping rules—you don't argue, you adapt. But I was wishing she would leave—Jerry was better at salving my wounds. At five o'clock a voice over the intercom announced that dinner was now being served in the day room. The hall became a freeway for wheelchairs, some racing like stock cars, and others chugging along like Model Ts. "Do you want to go?" Jerry asked.

"Oh no, I'm exhausted. I'll wait for them to bring my tray in here."

But instead, the perky Mrs. Allen appeared. "Your dinner is getting cold," she announced.

"Uh, I'd like my tray brought in here, please."

"Sorry. Everyone eats together in the day room."

"I don't want to go in there," I stormed. "I can't feed myself!"

"Here, I'll take…" Mama started.

"No! I don't want to go. I'm not hungry, anyway." Mama's hands were on her hips now. Jerry blew out a puff of air.

Mrs. Allen positioned herself behind my chair and began sifting strands of my hair through her fingers, as if she'd done this before. "I know you can't feed yourself today," she said softly, "but you'll learn to feed yourself. You don't want your family to have to feed you from now on, do you?"

*From now on?* Why didn't she just fork my heart out of my chest like a piece of meat and slice it with each comment? No one at the hospital made remarks like "from now on." Implications of the possibility, maybe, like the vocational-rehab gentleman, but certainly not blatant insinuations that I would be a from-now-on burden on the people I loved. And for her information, "from now on" wasn't listed as a choice for consideration. But to my utter displeasure, Mama announced, "She'll be right there," and marched like a sergeant beside Jerry as he pushed me to the huge room where my cold food waited.

Upon entrance into their day room, the stench of hospital food attacked my senses with a wave of nausea. A mélange of wheelchair-bound victims mirrored what I had refused to look at from the onset of this nightmare: quadriplegics being fed by nursing assistants or family members, braver ones struggling to feed themselves with specially devised utensils, and the fortunate paraplegics, who had only lost the use of their legs. I knew Mrs. Allen was trying to push me out of the nest, but I wanted to evaporate and fly into the clouds. I couldn't be fed in front of all these people like it was the normal thing to do. My fears were as real as my inability to cope with reality; I feared losing creditability for status in life as Jerry's wife and Kip's mother. I feared dehumanization.

Recognizing my sobs as the kind that would not dry up gracefully, Jerry left Mama stirring around in the uneaten food—as if doing so might make it desirable—and sped me back to my room. Once inside he touched the swinging red ball and asked for help to get me into bed, where I collapsed from what had been an exasperating day.

Mama left Jerry to deal with my fragility until the eight o'clock announcement for visitors to leave. Then, as I lay waiting for Jessie's arrival at eleven, I contemplated Mrs. Allen's comment, the rigidity of the schedules here, and concluded that Dr. Berkley's referral to my picnic being over might not have been such a far-fetched comparison after all. I was enduring the brace because there was no alternative, but could I endure the grueling schedules and restrictions of this institution? I'd based my entire life on my physical abilities: job, talents, sports, hobbies, and everyday functions. My posture, gestures, and gait were a intregal part of who I was. Could I leave this room with a mobile chair replacing the legs that were born to run? Could I face the world with hands that, at present, were just there? Not to mention my appearance. Flat, greasy hair and no makeup wasn't me. If my jeans were crooked, who, out of so many to care for, would have time to straighten them?

\* \* \*

Thinking took on a new dimension after that. My prayer life did, too. I'm ashamed to say that until I saw the daily struggle of a once-brilliant young man recuperating from a brain injury, I hadn't considered how thankful I should be that I could still do both. I'd been spoiled, but here tears won no merits—there were too many of us. The little-girl spirit stayed with me for the long haul, but being thrust among other patients with disabilities was the best thing that could've happened at this point. It was a slow process, but as the days rolled into weeks, I discovered what few on the "normal" side of life's spectrum ever absorb: life consists of more than the physical. Much more.

I swallowed my pride a bite at a time and learned to feed myself with an oversized spoon attached to a Velcro cuff strapped on my wrist. The brace prevented my head from meeting my hand half way, so raising my right arm was a painful, but rewarding experience. And if I got lucky, some of the food stayed on the spoon long enough to make it to my mouth. The hard work required to learn simple tasks taught me that unkempt hair and crooked jeans were trivialities. I met many talented, intelligent people who couldn't move a finger. But they could communicate. They could love. And those who recognized their potential still had much to contribute to society—sometimes more.

Before leaving each night, Jerry would turn the thermostat down low the way I liked it; and if I were too exhausted to watch TV, he'd turn out the lights and shut the door. It never got easy watching him leave to join our son at Ann's house, but with God's help I was committing to the inevitable. As I faced the darkness, I sensed an unseen guest hovering near. Without him, I would not have been able to endure the continual intrusions of the light being abruptly turned on in my face, or the trial-and-error procedures administered by unskilled aides who were forced to help because there was so many of us.

As for the dangling red ball, well, it had a mind of its own, but socking it was easier with the gigantic plastic splints I had to wear on my hands at night to keep my fingers straight. Even when it worked, I learned that waiting was part of the process. And I could scratch my nose with the splint on my right hand—something you can't appreciate unless you've experienced an unreachable itch.

Revelation comes when streams of light seep through the dungeon of adversity. Things like: the absence of people is not what renders one lonely, and darkness is no big deal if there is a candle burning in your heart. The Apostle Paul in II Corinthians 1:3–4 spoke of God as being *...the God of all comfort; who comforts us in all our tribulation, that we may be able to comfort them which are in any trouble, by the comfort wherewith we ourselves are comforted of God.* Adversity may not be *from* God, but he certainly can use adversity to equip us through it to help others.

The word *young* or *youth* implies more than the number of days we've lived; it's where naivety, innocence, and unharnessed zeal habitat. Imagine the potential if it were saved for the wisdom of a more-experienced life! Twenty-six was well past any innocent stage, but naivety and unharnessed zeal worked with my inbred stubbornness to get me over many hurdles, especially if I thought I needed to prove somebody wrong. An older me doesn't always have the oomph to accomplish something for the sake of proving a point, and I can see where rebellion has lengthened the life of lessons to be learned. I wrote a poem for my brother, Mark, when he graduated from high school. Part of it says it all:

> *You live and learn, they'll tell you*
> *But I think it's safe to say:*
> *If you will learn before you live*
> *It will soften up the way.*

Honesty demands to show its face here: I was not, never have been, probably never will be thankful for adversity. But I am thankful for the revelation of what's really important in life. And I'm thankful for God's faithfulness. On nights when loneliness and darkness couple up to launch an attack, I have a personal reference to the fact that I am never alone.

# 9

# A TYPICAL DAY

*This is the day the Lord hath made; we will rejoice and be glad in it.*
—Psalms 118:24

THERE ARE TWO KINDS of men—Esaus and Jacobs. I married an Esau—a cunning hunter and man of the field—and Esaus begat Esaus; it's that simple. Hang around them for a while, and in spite of your purposeful effort to subdue it, jargon known only to this brand of male will seep in. For instance, if he says he spotted "Grandpa" in the woods, you know it was a buck with an impressive spread. If he holds his hands up beside his head with fingers spread and a grin on his face when he tells it, well, it was either a monster or a doozy of a tale created by his wishful thinking while perched in a treestand in freezing weather.

You know when bucks are "in velvet": their antlers are covered in a velvet-like substance that they shed each year. And you know when they're "in rut": it's mating season.

Your eyes involuntarily train themselves to spot "scrapes": little trees that bucks have scraped their antlers on. And you can readily denote a "pawing": a pawed out place in the dirt seasoned with buck urine. Both performances are manly attempts to trumpet claim to their turf.

And if you've looked at, looked past, dusted, and prayed for a flood to wash the stuffed deer heads into a creek for more years than you care to imagine, you probably know which from his collection is considered a "nontypical." Ours is Kip's twelve-pointer with a drop point, which would have been something to brag about if the buck hadn't broken off one of his laurels in a jealous rage over a "dos-a-do."

It's amazing how the structure of what we consider typical can be restructured like dice in a gambler's hand and, given time, the activities of a nontypical day can become typical. Even "rehab talk" differs somewhat from "hospital talk," and you pick it up quickly, especially if it pertains to you. I refused to embrace phrases like "permanent quad" or permanent anything, but I learned to blend for the sake of those administering care to all of us, and for my own sanity. But there were days when I'd have traded my birthright for a cup of normality.

\* \* \*

It's seven o'clock Monday morning. You're not exactly chipper. You said goodbye to the weekend at eight o'clock last night when half of your reason to keep pressing on had to leave. You released the other half from your arms earlier Sunday afternoon, but not before you felt his young skin touch your lips and you photographed his smile in your mind. It will be a long week.

The dread of a typical day vexed your sleep like an undercurrent troubling the sea. You've not had normal sleep since you've been here, and it's needed for strength to work toward building back your crumbled temple. But undisturbed sleep is not on the schedule. It doesn't matter if you're dead to the world, every Sunday night between 11:00 p.m. and 1:00 a.m. the weighing ritual begins. "Why?" you ask. There's no rational answer. It's on their list of things to do, and so it's done.

Two of your assailants, dressed in starched-white uniforms, who had a Sunday afternoon nap and are eager to splash their weekend events back and forth across your never-mind-her body, hoist you onto a cold, flat scale, which they wheeled into your room on a gurney. Charting your weight—not your rest—is the issue, and they care little that you view them as Nazis in a prison camp. They ditto the same ninety-two pounds on the chart as last week, the week before, and ever since this ritual began.

One dump and your defenseless limbs sprawl into the warm bed, where you shiver with relief as they try to "make you comfortable" before attacking the next victim. You lie there, wide awake, still wondering why this procedure has to be done at all, much less in the middle of the night.

About the time you feel your body slipping into the deep sleep it craves, the heavy-breathing, overweight, older nursing assistant materializes like a creature in the night to use your body to practice the catheterization process. And again, you ask yourself why. Why do they allow aides, who don't seem to know where a female's waterworks are or how it operates, to perform such a tedious, private procedure? You have nothing against her personally, but your emotions are as tight as an over-wound watch. Emptying bladders is important, but you still feel violated. You even wonder if you're made right—this shouldn't be like threading a needle, should it? But if you complain, you'll lengthen the process, so you just fake sleep to avoid the shame.

As the night progresses, bang-bangs from John Wayne movies and laughter from Johnny Carson jokes jolt you periodically. You'd think the place would quieten down at some point. With all the rules, a TV curfew would not seem unreasonable, or at least a volume regulation. But even when the noise from other rooms fades, the cycle of around-the-clock activity continues. Just as you start to drift, the room door flings open and light invades your senses. Your feel your bed raising: it's time for more pills. "Would you like a sleeping pill?" the unsuspecting nurse asks.

*Yes, ten!*

When she has satisfactorily administered a paper cup full of capsules, she exits, leaving the door open behind her.

You bob for the ball swinging over your head to ask her to return and close the door, but no one answers. You bob again, this time with enough fervor to keep it swinging for some time.

"Can I help you?"

You tactfully voice your complaint. Ten minutes and a single snore later, you hear the door shut, only to be opened again, and again. If thoughts could kill...

At 4:00 a.m. the person pouring ice into a Styrofoam water pitcher might as well be a trumpeter; the place knows no mercy. You'd be willing to weave baskets with your teeth on the psychiatric ward if they'd let you get some sleep.

By 6:00 a.m. you're comatose. The electrifying intercom voice summoning personnel here and there doesn't even affect you. You've had one good hour of sleep.

The chief of this noble rehabilitation tribe bombards your tepee without exception at 7:00 a.m. each day. Unfortunately, your end-of-the-hall locale means you're first on his list.

The first-shift head nurse minding her p's and q's flips the light on and your eyebrows touch your lips. "Why is it so cold in here?" shouts the chief. And the head nurse shimmies to the thermometer like it's some tribal sin to sleep in a cool room. An intern with his eye on the chief's headpiece trails him like a shadow.

"How are you this morning?" asks the chief, looking over his glasses. But you can't make your tongue work. He gives your worn, brown security blanket your husband brought from home a jerk and you're uncovered down to your feet.

Oh, how you wish he wouldn't do that!

He examines your heels first, spying for potential bedsores with the fervency of a pest controller, and then rolls you onto your side and yanks down your underpants. *I thought the injury was in my neck,* you would like to say, before he pulls them up with a pop.

"Look's good," he reports.

Later in the day you might consider that a compliment.

\* \* \*

As voices fade and the temperature rises, you lapse back into the dream world you were in before "the awakening." The best time to sleep is right after dawn; you've always said that. But your ecstasy is short-lived. A voice as shrill as a cricket's brings you back.

"Goood morning," she proclaims.

*Oh Lord,* you pray under your breath, *not another student nurse!* But it's too late, she's here and you are her assignment.

"Hi, I'm Kathy," she smiles and says.

"Sandra," you mumble.

"What's that?"

"Uh, Sa…Sandra, my name is Sandra."

"Hi, Sandra, I'm Kathy," she repeats. "Your breakfast is here, now what do I do first, feed you, or do you do it, or what?"

Covering your head and deleting this day would feel good right now, but she's at your mercy as much as you are her's. "I need to sit up first, Kathy."

"Oh," she says, and then cranks up the head of your bed, stands back with hands in front of her chest like a begging puppy, and observes that you're slumped like a sack of potatoes.

"You'll have to pull me up," you say. So the poor thing pulls in every direction until you move an inch or two toward a sitting position, and then stands back and waits for further instructions.

"If you'll get my food ready, I can feed myself," you direct her. So Kathy briskly opens the milk carton and douses your coffee to the color of taffy.

"Whoa," you say. "Will you put a straw in my coffee, please?" And she jumps on it like a sprinter at takeoff.

You hold up your splinted hands, "I need these off." As she uncuffs you, you can see the enthusiasm in Kathy's face. You're the first patient in her apprenticeship and she can't wait to fulfill her calling to help people. You finish your breakfast and the fun begins.

"I'd like to brush my teeth before my bath."

"Sure." She wets your toothbrush, dabs toothpaste on it, and then points it in your direction.

"I can't handle that yet."

"Oh...uh."

"You'll need to get something for me to spit in."

"Spit in, spit in..." She retrieves a disposable cup from the holder by the sink. You open your mouth like a baby bird and she gets the hands-on experience of brushing a patient's teeth. Everything goes well until Kathy makes the mistake of positioning the pitcher of ice water over your body while pouring it into the cup. You let out a little yep when the lid comes off and you're baptized—ice and all. Kathy shoves a fist into her mouth. Her eyes are beginning to glaze over as she scrounges for a towel in the bathroom and starts to apologize.

"It's okay," you tell her. "Just get this gown off of me!" It opens in the back so that's not hard. "Uh, Raymond picks me up to take me to therapy at nine," you remind her. It's already 8:15 a.m. Kathy is clearly flustered, so you ask if she has a boyfriend; that usually helps. Color comes back to her face at the mention of his name—Michael. "Tell me about him," you say, as if the man of her dreams is your prime concern while you're naked and freezing. But you've got her relaxed, and that's the important thing.

You realize somewhere between Michael's new job and their wedding plans that time is slipping away and your sponge bath has only reached mid-body. "Kathy," you interrupt, "we'd better hurry."

Kathy glances at her huge white-banded wristwatch, gasps, and then swats the rest of your body with a bath cloth. She grabs your bra off the chair and flips you onto your side. You flop back like a rubber doll. She flips you again, this time holding your back with one hand, while digging under your side for the other end of your bra. She fastens it, and then slides it under the brace that extends like a cumbersome metal V between your shoulder blades. She releases her hand from your back and realizes the cups are stretched over the brace in front, closer to your chin than their intended focal point. "Oops," says Kathy, before yanking it down and securing it under the brace and then tucking your breasts in place.

She reaches for your hot-pink and black psychedelic blouse, and then thrusts you forward. Her schooling kicks in: she lays the opened blouse on your back, and then lets you gently fall back on it. She stuffs your arms into the blouse, tucks it under the brace, and then buttons it from the bottom up.

There's a knock at the door.

"Just a minute," she shouts. She starts cramming your feet into your jeans.

"Wait," you say, and she yanks them off.

"Where are…"

"They're in the wardrobe."

She scrambles for a pair of panties, blowing a straggling strand of hair off her forehead and you notice her hazel eyes glazing over again.

Raymond knocks the second time.

"Hey Raymond?" you holler.

The tall black man you've made friends with answers, "Yeah?"

"Can you come back in thirty minutes?"

"No problem," answers Raymond—he's used to it.

Kathy sighs. "Thanks." You can read her mind: She never knew it would be this hard; she's even questioning if this is her true calling, after all. Her nurse's cap that she proudly wears to represent her institute of learning is lopsided, and pieces of her dark hair are wandering aimlessly on her neck.

"So, when did you say you and Michael are getting married?"

Michael. You watch the tension leave her neck.

"June fourteenth," she says, stacking your jeans around your ankles like denim Slinkys.

When Raymond returns you're in your chair and ready for transfer. "See you tomorrow, Kathy," you say. She doesn't know it, but she's your assignment, too.

\*   \*   \*

Raymond parks you in line with other patients waiting for therapists to get to them, and you observe. The older man is a stroke victim—flowing tears give him away. So is the woman on the mat. You think of your grandparents and hope they never have to suffer from a stroke; these people should be enjoying their retirement years. You wish you could help.

And then there's Skip, struck down during his teens by a swimming accident. *He should be on the basketball court with his friends right now,* you think. You watch him balk at his therapist's suggestions and wonder if he'll grow out of his rebellion and stop blaming everybody else for his misery. And the even younger Jackie, who was at the wrong place at the wrong time when bullets were flying. What kind of life will he have? For your own sake, you've got to let it go and fight your own battles. Still, you ponder the significance of it all.

Debbie finishes up with Jackie, positions his wheelchair beside the mat, and then stands by as he transfers himself. *At least he has use of his arms and hands,* you think. That's to his advantage.

Debbie has been with you from the beginning. She wears her dark hair in a typical seventies' style: long, straight, and parted in the middle. It tickles your face as she transfers you to the mat Jackie left. She never shows her teeth when she smiles, and her face turns pink if you look her in the eye. She's deplete of make-up, and her only attention-getter is her crucifix. You feel bonded with Debbie because she saw you when you came in—a wreck from a wreck.

You wish sometimes she'd be more aggressive with the workout, though. A "come on, you can do it" with the words right down over the muscle she wants to move like a trainer in a boxer's face would help. But Debbie is the same: same tone, same moves, same expressions. But she witnessed your Palestine experience, and her comment about your condition "having to plateau," places a responsibility on your back. You don't know much about Catholicism, but you feel a responsibility to prove to her that *your high priest* hears you, and that you can come boldly into his presence, and that he—Jesus—is a trustworthy advocate just as the book of Hebrews says.

On the mat, Debbie lifts your right leg, holding your foot with one hand, pressing your knee with the other. Then she bends your knee, bringing your foot inward toward your face. She does this several times before positioning herself behind your foot and pushing it toward you until it dances. Bilateral ankle clonus is typical in a spinal injury.

After giving all four limbs a proper stretch, Debbie pinpoints specific muscles, holding her fingers on them like one would feel for a pulse. She smiles and says, "good," when she denotes activity that even you can't feel. You wonder why she can't visualize you whole. You hear her saying "plateau" in your sleep.

After a no-contest arm wrestle, she gets you back into your chair and wheels you next door to occupational therapy, where Gail awaits. Gail has the same long, parted-in-the-middle do, but hers is naturally curly and chestnut, and she pins it back. You like Gail, but you hate the way you're reduced to playing with toddler's toys and the childlike games. "Close your eyes and tell me which finger I'm touching," she instructs. You can feel some sensation, but you can't detect which finger she's touching with a Q-Tip or cotton ball. She lays a child's Tupperware ball on the table in front of you, and tells you to try to pick up the different-shaped objects and fit them into the correct holes. You think about swishing a basketball in the net from center court and both corners and you shake your head in disbelief at how difficult this is. You want to scream, to drop kick the toy in the nearest toilet bowl!

"Okay, good," says Gail, and then pulls Raggedy Ann out of her box of goodies. You'd like to rip Raggedy Ann's orange curls into shreds, but instead you swallow your pride and struggle to snap her snaps and zip her zipper. *How can these be the same fingers that punched numbers all day and played the piano?* Pity swells in your gut and glides upward, and you let it, because it's simply not fair.

You're thankful that your hour with Gail is only once a day. Your shoulders wrench from trying to hold your arms up to do the exercises. Gail wheels you into the hall, where Raymond picks you up and carries you back to your room on the third floor.

The lunch call comes, but you'd rather sleep.

\*   \*   \*

Raymond is back by 3:00 p.m. to carry you downstairs for another round of physical therapy. You've had a brief rest and catheterization, but your haggard body has little left by afternoon. You go through the motions, but Debbie does most of the work. When she transports you to Jim's office at 4:00, you can barely count to ten much less do fractions. Although you join your colleagues in utter disdain for these daily academic tests, for Jim's sake you try to show up—many don't bother. He can't help it if his job is to show you in black and white how ignorant you are. Housework, PTA, and keypunching hasn't exactly necessitated the use of algebra and geometry, and that side of your brain has always seemed somewhat fallow, so you forgot a lot of it. What's the big deal?

But it's on the list, and by George you're not an item skipper! So you allow Jim to fold your fingers around the fat pencil reserved for people like you, and when he looks at his time watch and says, "Go," you give it your best shot. Later, when the weeks of testing are over, you'll consider the irony of it when Jim gathers his data and informs you that you'd be best suited doing the type of work you were doing before the accident. You'll tell him to give you your hands back and you'll be happy to go back to your job, and then like a turtle out of water, you start inching your way toward the elevator with little toe pushes energized by the poignant reminder that you're crippled *and* dumb. He'll say that he wishes he could give you your hands back, and to let him push you, but when you tell him you'd like to try it alone, he'll understand. The thirty minutes it will take you to get to the elevator down the hall will give you a good squalling space.

\*    \*    \*

By late afternoon on a typical day you watch stacks of smoke from downtown factories meet the clouds from the day room window. You get a whiff, sweet like a pipe, from one of the RJ Reynolds plants, and you think of your grandma's Tuberose snuff. Hanes Mall across the street is lit up with early Christmas lights. You relive dashing in and out of the different shops and the escalator rides—so new and different from the familiar shopping centers. You remember when downtown Fourth Street was where you shopped—a once-a-year extravaganza for school clothes—and the anticipation felt when you stepped on the elevator at L. Roberts or Arcade and said, "Third please," to the elevator operator. A club sandwich and Coke from Walgreens topped your day. The simplicity of that era slipped away when shopping centers replaced downtown shopping. And now the shops are all under a single roof, and you wish you were there like the rest of the world, drinking in the preparatory sounds and smells of Christmas.

Jackie and a boy visiting him are driving colored balls with numbers into pockets with cue sticks from their wheelchairs in the center of the room. Skip dashes in and out in his two-wheeler, as if staying on the move would deaden the pain of the absence of family. They live out of town, but you wonder if they know how long it is from weekend to weekend in this place.

Mrs. Nuckles is in her usual spot in front of the day room TV. Her silver hair atop smooth paper-sack-colored skin puts you in mind of whipped cream on hot chocolate. Rumor has it that she came from good stock in Winston, mingling with the Grays and Reynolds, maybe. Her mind allows her to live only in the present, and at the present Fred Sanford has just caused her to spew out the "n" word, as if her current state of mind gives her permission to poke fun at her own race. You enjoy her from a distance, because you were close at hand the day she threw a whole plate of food in another patient's face for no apparent reason.

Nolan wheels himself over to make conversation. Maybe it's because you don't have to look up, or he isn't looking down. Or maybe it's because you've grown enough to consider him a comrade rather than a reminder of the way you are. Whatever the reason, you enjoy learning about his life, telling him about yours.

You watch the elevator door as one might when expecting the Prize Award van from Publisher's Clearing House. When it finally opens and reveals the man whose smile is worth more than a million dollars, you feel like you could jump up and run to him, but you know you can't, so you watch him walk to you, and the load of the day's toil lifts.

He picks at Mrs. Nuckles, edging her on to see if some eccentric comment might roll off her tongue. It does, and you laugh out loud for the first time today. When he has to leave, you strain to hear the sound of his shoes meet the hard tile floor before it trails into a memory and all you have left is the smell of his aftershave on your hands.

\* \* \*

Such is a typical "nontypical" day at John C. Whitaker Rehabilitation Center. Not that I'm complaining. They were the hoeing and weeding days. The days when you wipe sweat from your brow and pray for rain. Your muscles ache, but your heart is hopeful. Sometimes the wind blows away yesterday's progress, and you wonder if all is in vain. And then the sun peaks through the clouds with new mercy, and you stretch yourself until it hurts, knowing every harvest has its price. If this crop is sabotaged, it won't be by you. You endure the nontypical and promise yourself that you'll never take another typical day for granted. As a matter of fact, in your mind, an ordinary day now ranks among the extraordinary. And any sunset will do.

# 10

## THANKSGIVING

*In everything give thanks, for this is the will of God in Christ Jesus concerning you.* —I THESSALONIANS 5:18

> *In your eyes I see loneliness*
> *Looking straight at me*
> *In your eyes I see sorrowfulness*
> *Wanting it to flee*
> *In your eyes I see tenderness*
> *Wishing I'd agree*
> *In your eyes I see emptiness*
> *As hollow as a tree*
> *In your eyes I see loneliness*
> *Looking straight at me*

AS A SMALL-TOWN CLASS of no more than sixty students who started out in the first grade together, we were like berries in a cobbler—close-knit and similar. East Bend School was both an elementary and a high school, so the majority of us had been together for eleven years now. Others joined us from Fall Creek and Forbush Elementary in the ninth grade. The worst things we ever did were skip class now and then, throw spit wads, smooch on break, and I'm sorry to say, copy each other's paper on occasional. Discipline wasn't a problem—our parents punished us, not the teachers, if and when we needed correction.

The fire that demolished the auditorium, elementary classrooms, and half of the high school building our freshmen year united us even more—the whole school, for that matter. The hardest part of the loss for me was when the workmen drove nails into our hallowed gymnasium floor to put up temporary partitions for classrooms. Coach Jim Morgan had kept our gym floor in mirror condition and disciplined anyone who dared to step on it with street shoes. Thankfully, the fire happened during the night and no one was injured. But it hurt my heart to sit in Algebra and look up at the netless goal tucked under like a bowed head. I'd waited forever, it seemed, to try out for the girl's basketball team, and now that I'd finally made it, we had to load up on the activity bus after school each day and practice at Fall Creek's tiny gym and cafeteria combination. It wasn't even a full court, and the stench of garbage cans full of discarded lunch food made unpleasant conditions for practicing. But we held on to each other and the promise of a new building and a refinished gym floor by the time the next school year rolled around.

Norm Barnes wore many hats at East Bend High School. In addition to teaching junior and senior English, directing the senior play, coordinating the senior trip to Washington and New York City, and heading up the cheerleading squad, Mr. Barnes directed our traveling Glee Club. We performed at area church services and revival meetings singing songs such as, "My Sheep Know My Voice," and "Great Is Thy Faithfulness." We also sang songs like "Drink to Me Only with Thine Eyes" and "Love Is a Many Splendored Thing"—songs he grew up on—at school functions. Having Mr. Barnes like you was equivalent to finding favor with deity, or so we thought. And I had to earn his approval, because he clearly didn't like me until I reached his English class in the eleventh grade, where I worked hard to prove myself worthy of his esteem. Comments from him, when and where he made them, and if they made me shrink or soar are imprinted on my mind like initials carved on a tree.

Jerry, on the other hand, came to East Bend High School from Fall Creek Elementary with a don't-mess-with-me attitude. I watched him walk right out of World History class in the tenth grade knowing he'd have to take it over the next year. He still maintains it's because the teacher grossed him out by blowing his nose all the time. Mr. Barnes kept telling him to grow up, and even wrote it in the back of one of his yearbooks.

Like most of us, Jerry struggled with articulation. I believe it had something to do with locale (living in the sticks) as much as age. And we all were sensitive and easily embarrassed. Status and approval were unspoken ambitions in our day, and talking back to a teacher was rare. I recall Mr. Williams asking me (in typing class, I think) to define the word "strategy" in one of his classes. I knew what it meant, but I simply couldn't articulate it in front of everyone. I can count on one hand the books I read in high school, which might have contributed to my lack of communication skills. I waded through Ernest Hemmingway's *The Old Man and the Sea* so I could write a book report. A book called *The Shakers* about two lovers who were separated by a religious cult held my attention and stirred up a few hormones, though.

Everyone came to school pressed and proper. I've got a picture of a bunch of us in the tenth grade dressed in what was supposed to be a "messy garb" for Beta Club initiation. Looking at it now, the only thing that looks messy is Steve Coram's shirttail outside his pants. My hair wasn't as teased as usual and I had a big bow in it, but other than that we looked like nerds fast-forwarded to the eighties.

The boys wore oxford cloth button-down shirts in pastel colors—even pink—with socks to match, wingtips, or loafers. Tennis shoes were for the basketball court. It was common to see the guys with jackets in various colors. Jerry had a pale yellow one that got my attention. Pants were creased, without pleats, and fit snuggly. The Beatles haircut hadn't taken off in East Bend, but we were usually behind when it came to styles and fads. The guys wore short cuts, combed straight down on the forehead or parted to one side. I don't recall beards or mustaches, maybe a little stubble if a week passed without shaving, God forbid. English Leather cologne was hot—real hot.

The fair coming to town in the fall signaled time for us girls to start wearing our wool skirts and sweaters. Bass Weejuns (in burgundy, green, navy, black, or brown) or simple flats were the footwear. By the time the boys started practicing baseball, we'd switch to cotton. We wore pantyhose held up by garter belts or girdles, and bobby or knee socks. Matching underwear was cool. Or was it groovy? Actually, I think it was neat, because nifty would have been passé. The point is, we liked to match down to the skin. Hair was teased and stiff, flipped up or under, piled on top of our heads, or in a French twist if it was long enough. We never wore pants to school, and I don't remember owning jeans until the seventies. Go-go boots were big about the time Nancy Sinatra came out with "These Boots Were Made for Walking."

The guy whose class ring had been waxed to my finger since I was a freshman was now a college student. Richard Thomas was six-foot four and we looked like Mutt and Jeff, but he had captured my heart from the basketball court. That he would give me, a measly freshman (and squirt), the time of day was exciting. He was my first "real" boyfriend and we were great friends. Our days together as sweethearts closed my junior year, but he invited me to hold a concert years later at a church he was pastoring—he's now a Baptist minister. I'll never forget how the Lord kept impressing upon me to share about marital faithfulness—Jerry and I had just gone through a painful ordeal. I did more sharing than singing. I'm not sure if Richard was happy about my speech or not; he was under doctor's orders at the time not to even step into the pulpit. But I can tell you, Jerry was not happy about it at all. On the drive home he wore my ears out. "People don't want to hear you preach! You were invited to sing!" But in spite of his displeasure, Richard's wife and my classmate and friend, Mary Ruth, told me later that an incident happened to one of their members shortly afterward, and the woman was sure my message was for her.

But in 1965 I was just sixteen, and Richard was out of sight. And don't gag, but every time I looked up Jerry's magnetic blue eyes were looking into mine. Honestly, they had an unusual drawing power. And on this particularly sad autumn day, I couldn't ignore them.

Jerry's sister, Linda, and her young family had been victims of an auto accident while on their way to work. Linda's husband, Lynn, was driving as Linda held their eleven-month-old baby, Todd, in her lap. (Child seats were not mandatory.) They were en route to Lynn's parents' house to leave Todd when an illegal immigrant driving a stolen car ran a stop sign and hit them broadside. Lynn was pronounced DOA at the hospital, and the baby was barely holding onto life. Linda was treated with minor injuries and released.

Bad news travels like wildfire in a small town, so the moment I saw Jerry's dad's white Ford Galaxy 500 pull into the parking lot at the gymnasium at the morning break, my heart led me toward him. We spoke briefly, and then the bell summoned me to Mr. Barnes' English class. Of course, when Mr. Barnes gave us the assignment to write a poem, many wrote about the accident—everyone knew them. But all I could think about was Jerry's eyes, sad and piercing.

That night after I got home from basketball practice, my mom— very pregnant with Mark—came to my room and announced that some guy named Jerry was asking if he could see me. My heart fell. What could I say to him? Death had not touched me in such an intimate way. His visit was short, but long enough to communicate his need for my friendship. To add sorrow upon sorrow, Jerry lost his nephew, Todd, the next day.

*  *  *

I've seen that same look of pain in Jerry's eyes over the years, and each time I'm just as stricken by a need to heal them. Ten years and a million words later my poem was just as relevant. Only now we were married with a child. Fatigue had etched a road map above those eyes I'd learned to love, and I was selfishly dumping on him my ache to see his face on a daily basis. And he was there for me, as fervently faithful as he was dramatically impulsive the day he walked out of World History. I think Mr. Barnes unofficially stamped him grown up after everyone saw that he just might stick it out with me.

Despite that seeing Jerry each night graced me with enough stamina to get me through another twenty-four hours, I released him to take one night off each week from coming to see me. Wasn't I generous? But I'll have to admit, he wasn't easily persuaded. It seemed he needed to see me, also, and to witness my daily progress. Maybe because my progress was also his. He needed to touch me, if it meant only the back of his hand brushing my face like a leaf kissing the wind before it falls. He needed to fill the gap where my affliction failed me. Because we were one.

"Do something you've always wanted to do," I told him. But when he told me what that something was, my mouth flung open tunnel-like and hung there until I could echo, "Banjo lessons?"

"Well, I've always wanted to learn to play the banjo."

He had? I guess even the closest two can't know the other's deepest inward desires. He purchased a banjo and made arrangements to take lessons every Tuesday night from Ed Easter of The Easter Brothers, a bluegrass gospel group. I don't think Jerry will mind me telling you that he never advanced past "Cripple Creek" plucked out one sluggish note at a time, but it gave him a much-needed change of pace. And the drive to Mount Airy (the real Mayberry of "The Andy Griffith Show") provided solitude for his cluttered mind. I still think he could have done it if he'd been as dedicated to practicing as he was to hunting and fishing, but there's more to becoming proficient on an instrument than a weekly lesson and a cassette tape filled with banjo runs. Not to mention, free time to pick and grin was scarce.

Unfortunately, Jerry couldn't seem to focus on the deer hunting he loved, either; and I felt guilty that his prospects for a big buck were ruined because of me. Ever since we'd been together, I'd longed for him to choose family over hunting on Thanksgiving Day. But Jerry thought the holiday was to celebrate the male pilgrim's ability to stalk wild game, while the women and children sat patiently on a big rock named after a car. Believe me, I've sulked through many Thanksgiving holidays, because I'd always had the impression that love, marriage, and special occasions intertwined. But coming of age brought with it the shattering of youthful ideals. My search for the romantic side of traditions was like cracking a decorated egg just to find it had rotted. Our conflicting ideas resulted in something like rubbing a cat's hair in the wrong direction. But regardless of my persuasive argument, Jerry spent the day—and usually the night—in a mountain shanty with his hunting buddies. And now that I had him all to myself, my conscience wouldn't let me take advantage of it.

"I want you to go hunting on Thanksgiving Day," I forced myself to tell him.

"No, I'm not interested this year. I want to be here with you. Besides, I don't even know where I'd go."

"Well, you'd might as well find a place, because I don't want you down here," I smirked.

"Yes, you do," he replied, touching my nose with the tip of a finger.

"No, I mean it. You're going hunting on Thanksgiving Day, and that's that."

He dropped his head. "We'll see."

"Look," I said, "Mama told me that Granny Hobson wants to send me a special lunch from her kitchen, so I agreed."

"Oh, you did?"

"Yes, I did. And I'd like to have lunch with Mama, so you might as well go deer hunting. I don't want to see your face Thanksgiving Day."

He gave me a dimpled grin. "I guess I could take Kip somewhere and let him hunt."

"Yeah." My eyes grew at the thought of Kip and Jerry doing something special together. "He'll love that!" I said. "So it's settled. You plan your day with Kip."

* * *

Thanksgiving in the day room at Whitaker wasn't a picture-perfect place for a family gathering, so I told myself it would be just another day. Mama would bring a picnic from Granny's table, we'd chat, and I'd survive without Jerry or Kip. I knew Kip would be excited about getting to sit in a treestand with his daddy. But when the last Thursday in November arrived, I tried to hide the dip in my spirit as the other patients' mates flocked in.

Even the nurses missed Jerry on the days he didn't show up. Especially Mrs. Allen, who Jerry quickly learned would render him invisible long after visiting hours if he left a pizza at the nursing station. He freed the nurses from my cosmetic ritual each night, and basically most of my other needs while he was there. His silver four-wheel-drive Jeep truck, we found out, was the topic of one of the Tuesday morning, "confidential" doctor and head nurse conferences. It seemed that one of the doctors on staff suspected it was Jerry's wheel prints on the creosote poles on each side of the token gate. Not much eluded my room, especially if it directly concerned me, and that piece of news was no exception—I knew it before Dr. Roberts made his afternoon rounds.

I'll let you decide if you think Jerry was the culprit, but I will say this: Jerry, and the rest of my family, deposited their share of fifty-cent pieces in that machine. And what would you do if the system was down and you're dog-tired with a thirty-minute drive ahead of you late at night and you're under the wheel of a silver monster with more than adequate crawling power? Rules have always ignited a spark of defiance in my husband, especially when they seem unreasonable.

Thanksgiving found Mama and me in the day room digging into a basket of Granny Hobson's home-cooked delicacies. And I must admit, this baked aroma awakened my dormant adrenaline glands with jaw-aching pleasure. I've been known to sneak my share of cold biscuits from Granny's kitchen through the years, and since my appetite for hospital food had long ago waned, I could use the calories. There was no therapy because of the holiday, so we had a leisurely lunch.

Throughout the meal, Mr. Talbot's face kept invading my thoughts. I'd noticed him in physical therapy for several days before we actually made conversation. I didn't ask, but his symptoms seemed typical of a stroke victim—paralyzed on one side, emotional, elderly. We were parked beside each other on the day we formally met, waiting for our turns on the mat. He seemed taken with me in a grandfatherly way. With moist eyes he reached and stroked my hand. "You're too young to be like this," he said.

I agreed, but I sensed that I should prove to him (quickly) that I was going to be fine. "Oh, it's okay. I can move my feet. See?" I demonstrated by lifting my left foot as high as I could off the footrest. My effort seemed to only fuel his concern. Crocodile tears were now wetting his shirt. *Oh no!* I panicked. *Help me, Lord.*

And he did. Mr. Talbot and I became friends. His curiosity gave me space to mention God's goodness as I explained the accident. But we were never left alone for very long. I wondered, as Mama and I ate Thanksgiving dinner, if he would have visitors for the holiday. And then it hit me: I could be a visitor, just in case no one else came.

"Mama, when we finish eating, I'd like to go up to the fourth floor," I told her.

"Okay. Who's up there you want to see?" I explained about Mr. Talbot, and after our meal, we headed for the elevator. I found Mr. Talbot in a four-bed ward and there were four sets of eyes glued to a football game on the TV suspending from the ceiling in the center of the room.

"Well, hello there," Mr. Talbot exclaimed, smiling broadly. "What brings you up here?"

"I've come to see you and wish you a happy Thanksgiving," I returned. "But I don't want to disturb the game."

"Ah, don't worry about that. I'm just watching it because it's on."

"Uh, Mr. Talbot, this is my mother, Ruth," I said. They exchanged greetings, and then without warning, Mama excused herself and left me with four men in pajamas. "You had company today?" I queried.

"Yes, earlier," was all I could get from him. We hee-hawed around, exchanging pleasantries, but I was wishing Mama would come back. I clutched the metal bar holding my chin brace in place with my good hand and pulled it down to free my head to turn slightly toward the door. I could feel the other men eyeballing me, and I needed to do whatever the Spirit had sent me up there for, and then get out.

The space between us demanded some conversation, and frankly, my mind could only conjure one approach. So out it rolled, raw and poignant: "Do you know Jesus, Mr. Talbot?" I was shocked at my own audacity. I gave the other men a sharp glare. Their eyes hopped back to the game like fleas on a dog. They were probably thinking I'd target them next. I was sure I'd blown it, but when those familiar tears welled up in my friend's eyes and tumbled down his ruddy cheeks, I knew something or someone had prepared him for this moment—I'd come to finish the job. Mr. Talbot shook his head, making my next question a breeze: "Would you like to?"

He simply replied, "Yes." So I prayed with him to receive the Lord in his heart.

Mama walked in the moment we said amen, as if she and I had synchronized watches. I said goodbye to Mr. Talbot and left. When I told her that the elderly man had just gotten saved, she said, "What? I wasn't gone but five minutes!" It seemed like an hour to me.

Mr. Talbot left the rehab center shortly afterward, and I never got to follow up on his decision. I knew nothing about his background or where he was from, but I believe God knitted us together for that day, that moment. I wasn't as equipped for witnessing as I should have been, but I had the most important element, the Holy Spirit, and he took up the slack. And I was bold. Lord, was I bold!

In all probability, Mr. Talbot has left this world by now, but in spite of my crude evangelistic approach, I expect to see him again one day. And you know, the two sets of blue eyes (Jerry's and Kip's) that were absent from my Thanksgiving celebration were replaced by melancholy eyes growing dim by time. And as I lay in bed that night, with the noise around me that had become home sounds, joy bubbles rose inside me. I would see those glassy gray eyes, hungry for what only Jesus could give him, for a long time in my memory. Like that sad Thanksgiving in 1965 after the loss of Lynn and Todd, this wasn't the Thanksgiving I'd planned. But out of my fifty-plus years, these are the two Thanksgiving seasons I look back on with bittersweet detail.

# 11

## CHRISTMAS

*And she shall bring forth a son, and thou shalt call his name Jesus: for he shall save his people from their sins.* —MATTHEW 1:21

EVEN WITH MY ATTEMPT to thwart its spell, Christmas was invading my senses. The woodsy smell of the Fraser fir in the day room. The hint of cinnamon from the Moravian cookies left at the nursing station. Hanes Mall lighted with commerce in plain view from the day room window. The massive star atop the hospital as a reminder of Bethlehem's stall with its kingly inhabitants. Poinsettias filling otherwise dull spaces with crimson color. And Salvation Army bells were ringing in distant public places. I knew they were, even though I couldn't hear them.

How dare Christmas come now, with me here! I wanted to undeck the halls, because I was anything but jolly. I wanted to revert, if only in my dreams, to Christmases past.

\* \* \*

*I was seven, eight at the most, when I arose early on Christmas morning and went directly to my parents' bedroom so Mama could brush my hair and get the Kodak ready. Peeping wasn't allowed, and I didn't know kids were expected to anyway. I guess when you don't have a sibling to imitate or compete with, you just do as you're told. I was wearing blue made-by-Hanes pajamas—I can still feel the soft cotton stretched over my skin. The sharp fragrance from the field-cut cedar in the living room penetrated the house, and the angel hair and silver tinsel sealed that old-timey Christmas feeling for recall. Under the tree sat a doll not over six inches tall named The Littlest Angel with a little granite-speckled tin wardrobe to closet her tiny clothes. Christmas was the most wonderful time of the year!*

\*   \*   \*

Time seemed to be the only thing moving with any normalcy, and I was wishing, praying that my body would catch up. Christmas and Kip had become one word. How could I be separated from my child at Christmas? Going home for visits, as I knew some patients had done, had not been discussed. My focus was going home period. But that hadn't been discussed, either. So the pretty young nurse, great with her own child, had no way of knowing she was about to send me into a tailspin.

"It will be spring when you go home, won't it, Sandra?"

"Spring?" I softly echoed, as images of sweaters peeling, lawnmowers cranking, and happy crocus popping colorful heads through yards carpeted with new grass proceeded to poke fun at my heart.

She refilled the Styrofoam pitcher on the nightstand with ice and water. "Yeah, your release date is set for March 15, isn't it?"

I tried to disguise the shock. "Oh, uh, I don't know. Dr. Martinat hasn't mentioned it."

He hadn't mentioned it and I hadn't asked. The soul's container can only hold so many emotions before the lid blows off, and mine was boiling. March would mean I'd not only be separated from Kip on Christmas, but his seventh birthday, and practically his whole first-grade school year! Thank God for tears. I held them until the unsuspecting nurse left. Then the enemy unpacked his bags on my shoulder and sang *Na, Na, Na, Na, Na. You can't go home for Christmas. You can't go home till spring. You can't go home until next year. You pitiful little thing.*"

\*   \*   \*

*"Now, this will be your last doll," Mama said. I don't know why she figured the fourth grade had to be the last year a girl should get a doll for Christmas. But Mama said it...*

*We had a movie camera by then, so Daddy got the lights attached while Mama brushed my hair, and then I made my grand entrance, where my last doll and a black King James Bible sat unwrapped under the tree. I couldn't fathom why it would matter if your hair was sticking up when you were still in your pajamas, but I'll hand it to Mama for this: Tootles was a fine doll for a finale. She was the size of a year-old baby and her eyes would shut when you laid her down. And I adored her. When the dress that came on her finally wore out, the rose-velvet dress Grandma Davis made for me and I'd had my picture made in when I was a baby fit her just fine. Mama paid Santa a bunch for Tootles, probably because she would be my last doll—which seemed to be set in stone. And as usual, Mama was right. If I'd got a doll for Christmas in the fifth grade, I'd have died!*

✳   ✳   ✳

I was still crying when Jerry put me to bed that night, and then left for home. I prayed when I could in between things being done, but I needed a human ear, too, someone who had an interest in what was going on. Our preacher friend Rev. Clyde Phillips had told me to call him if I ever needed to talk, so oblivious to the hands on the clock, I asked a nursing assistant to dial his number. When it rang, she laid the receiver between the pillow and my ear, and then exited.

A froggy "Hello" told me Clyde and Dot had already gone to bed. "Clyde?"

He recognized my voice. "Sandra, what's wrong?"

"I'm sorry, Clyde, I didn't realize how late it is."

"Oh, don't worry about that. We just laid down. Are you alright?"

Can't-help-it tears were still cascading like a downspout. "A nurse told me today that I'm not going to be released until March. Clyde, I can't stay here that long!"

"Now, you listen here." I sensed the eruption of a sermon. "Hasn't the Lord been with you so far? Huh? Now, hasn't he?"

I squeaked out a yes.

"Well, he's gonna see you through; he's not gonna leave you now."

Of course, I knew that God wouldn't abandon me, but just hearing it from Clyde helped it to penetrate. "I'm sorry I got you up. Tell Dot I'm sorry, too. I just needed to talk to you. Jerry and I appreciate you being here for us."

"You know what?" Clyde's voice broke. "Today's my spiritual birthday and your call is icing on my cake. I love Jerry and you, and I want you to know that I'll be here anytime either of you need me."

"Thanks, Clyde. We love you, too."

"You feel better?"

"Yeah, I guess I just needed to unload on somebody. You're special to us, Clyde."

"Hey, I don't think you know what an inspiration you've been to me, and a lot of others, too." I'd heard those words from so many people, and I felt blessed that God was using me, even in diverse circumstances. "Listen, I'll drop by tomorrow, I mean today." Clyde said with a chuckle, which made me visualize the laugh that had warmed me on many cloudy days.

"Okay, I'll see you then." I said. "And Clyde…"

"Yeah?"

"Happy birthday!"

\* \* \*

*I threw up all night from a stomach virus on Christmas Eve, so Mama slept with me. Just before dawn began to stretch over the horizon, I got sick again. Even with waves of nausea making me dizzy, I had to peek into the living room on my way back to bed—I hadn't heard a sound in there all night, and as much as I was up, I thought I would have detected it if there'd been any action. Mama let out a gasp when I opened the door, but it was too late. Through patches of darkness incoming moonbeams reflected off a shiny metallic blue bike—my first, my only. "There's a bicycle in there," I whispered, and then closed the door in respect to Christmas morning, which had not fully arrived, and climbed back into the warm spot beside my mama.*

\* \* \*

It's easy to tell yourself you can weather the storm, but it's another thing when the "glitter meets the load." Christmas was all around me, and all I could think about was home. I knew a miracle was required to persuade Dr. Martinat to let me go home for a few hours on Christmas Eve. Each time I pressed it, his answer was emphatically, "You're not ready." The hospital walls, grim as stale air, were closing in on me.

I watched other patients leave with family members on Saturdays and I ached to just take a short ride. But Dr. Martinat would see me from a distance and spit out, "No way!" I was beginning to wonder if I were destined to live, move, and breath at someone else's command. I'd moved from parental rules and teacher's rulers into a marriage situation, which was different, but I was still accountable for where I went and how I looked. And even my workplace at Western Electric resembled a classroom, with the boss at her desk peering over horn-rimmed glasses to see if I was talking to the person next to me. My spirit was screaming for freedom like a wild animal caught in a trap.

One day Dr. Martinat stopped to see if my chin brace was tight enough—I didn't seem to look as miserable as he thought I should. Jerry was with me when I reiterated, "Can't we shoot for a pass for Christmas Eve, Dr. Martinat?" He let out a deep sigh and the words I was growing accustomed to hearing started to form. But he made the mistake of looking directly into my eyes. "I've got a little six-year-old boy who wants his mama home for Christmas."

He paused and drew a long breath—I had him cornered. He turned to Jerry with an authoritative glare and asked the million-dollar question: "Can you learn to catheterize your wife by Christmas?" I'm sure he thought Jerry would back down from that one.

"Yes." Jerry retorted.

"Well, you've got two weeks to convince me. Then we'll talk." With that the doctor moved to the needs of another patient.

*    *    *

*Seventh grade was an awkward year. I was still a little girl to my parents, but I'd started my period, for goodness sake, so I thought I'd surely evolved to the first step of womanhood. Our class was rated the all-time-meanest-ever to bedevil East Bend School, so we had a reputation to uphold. My ponytail was gone, along with anything that might ruin my new, bad image. And if I learned anything, it was because Mrs. Winnie Hobson was a good teacher. But the day she asked the class who Sebastian Cabot was and I raised my hand and said, "Isn't he on TV?" I think I finally exasperated her.*

*So in keeping with the status quo, when Christmas rolled around, I informed my parents that I no longer believed in Santa Clause. In my heart of hearts I really wanted them to argue the point at least one more year, but Daddy immediately responded by saying he didn't see any sense in him having to get up in the middle of the night and traipse out in the cold if that were the case. So before bed, he retrieved my portable record player and new forty-fives from their hiding place in the trunk of the car. I figured surely Mama wouldn't let me down by dragging out all my presents, but I stupidly tested her by asking if there was anything else, anyway. A "no" to that would have sufficed, but she told me to look in her closet, like it wasn't a big deal. There I found a big white stuffed cat with blue glass eyes and a necklace around its neck.*

*I got what I'd asked for, but not necessarily what I'd really wanted. "Soldier Boy," "He's a Rebel," "I'll Do My Crying in the Rain," and "Duke of Earl," to name a few, temporarily tranquilized my growing pains. Parents should be sensitive to the fact that kids don't always want the true answers to their questions, though.*

\* \* \*

Mrs. Allen, now Cindi, closed the door to my room and demonstrated the mechanics of the cauterization process to my willing husband. Maybe it was because he was an electrician and experienced at handling live wires with delicacy, but God as my witness, he was gentler than any of the medical professionals. But then, his touch could never be reduced to a procedure. With some of the probing I had to endure, he should have taught a class!

It was the week before Christmas before the cautious doctor would agree to give me a three-hour pass on Christmas Eve, and then only if the weather was good. But when I awoke on the morning of Christmas Eve, the parking lot looked like an alabaster sea. The enormous flakes continued throughout the day like fluffy white feathers tumbling from a somber gray sky. The extended forecast predicted more of the same. Dr. Martinat hadn't left orders for a pass for me, but my essentials were packed for the trip when Jerry arrived that afternoon. Jerry could have taken me without the doctor's permission, but I was in good standing with the center—I didn't want to be defiant. And BlueCross BlueShield had kept us from going bankrupt. An accident without the doctor's permission to leave could have changed all that. So we waited until Dr. Martinat arrived late that evening for his rounds. To his displeasure, our faces were the first he saw upon exiting the elevator.

He started shaking his head. "It's too dangerous. You could have an accident." My countenance fell. Dr. Martinat squatted down beside my wheelchair and compassionately asked, "Do you want to risk having another injury after you've come so far?" My eyes answered. Even if the road leading home looked precarious, we were young and fearless, excited by the adventure. And I was dying to feel the wind in my face and to touch the elements of the world outside the perimeter of those sanitary walls. We might not have been using wisdom, but to us facing challenges seemed more like "living" than avoiding them to prevent something that might not happen. And the prize awaiting—seeing Kip and Mark—was well worth the risk.

The doctor held up both hands. "Okay," and then he asked Jerry what he already knew, "Are you in your truck?"

\* \* \*

*My sixteenth Christmas present came early. December 6, 1965 to be exact. I skipped school that morning to go with my parents to Forsyth Memorial Hospital, and it's a good thing I did—my bedazzled father couldn't even remember my age or Grandma Davis' maiden name when we were admitting Mama. I wondered if he was that nervous when I was born. I'll never forget Daddy's exuberance when they finally announced over an intercom in the fathers' waiting room that he had a son. And I'll never forget my groggy mom trying to fork food off of a reeling plate immediately after delivery. I think that woman could eat sitting on a dead horse! And as you'd expect, my brother was then the center attraction. Daddy took me to downtown Winston-Salem before Christmas and let me pick out a few outfits. I felt somewhat slighted, but having a baby brother made up for it. I just couldn't believe they waited until I was (nearly) grown to have him.*

\* \* \*

The acrid air bit my nose and cheeks when Jerry pushed me out the back entrance and loaded me into his pick-up like one would handle a fragile glass sculpture. He was all too aware of the responsibility that rested on his shoulders, but we plowed westward through eight inches of snow, with more falling, as if we had good sense. But then, what can deter two warriors empowered by the spirit of Christmas? Jerry and Ole Silver were known throughout the center for gallant displays, and he wasn't about to alter that reputation. And my heart was aimed for home like Grandpa Hobson's workhorse, Nell, used to head for the barn after a day of pulling tobacco sleds.

We passed more stalled cars on I-40 than moving ones, as we crept toward where the sun would be setting on a clear day. Any other time, Jerry would have stopped to assist people, but time allowed no other delays. Giant snowflakes exploded against the windshield with intensifying vigor as we finally exited and headed toward Yadkin County. It was an exhilarating ride. But we knew full well that returning to Whitaker in three hours was not plausible.

Jerry took his eyes off the road to glance my way as we passed the scarred pine that had brought Daddy's car to rein back in October. The accident sight gave me an eerie feeling, like I needed to stop and pick up something valuable. But the breathtaking beauty falling upon us had blanketed the sight with layers of purest white. And a deep gratitude for the gift of life and love produced eyes moistened instead with hope. Oaks, pines, and maples bowed in reverence to the weight of the heavenly powder. Candles glowed in the windows of country homes warmed by simmering logs and the magnitude of the season. I can't recall a winter storm quite as stimulating.

\* \* \*

*A borrowed silver foil tree with blue glass ball ornaments sat on the corner bar in our trailer during Christmas 1970. Money was scarce, but there was a little green peddle motorcycle, a cap-buster rifle with a sheriff's badge and a canteen (his father's choice), a See-N-Say by Mattel, and a one-engine train under the tree on Christmas morning. Twenty-one-month-old Kip didn't know but that we were well off, and we were, because love filled any void for things lacked materially. I was more than satisfied that nothing we would ever face would be too big as long as we had each other. And if God had let me hand pick my child's features, I would not have changed one. He was the most perfect being my eyes had ever beheld. If our marital union had no other purpose but to bring Kip into the world, that would have been enough. Touching him was like touching heaven, and every tear I dried and every smile I witnessed fulfilled me. Legal or not, how anyone could choose to destroy such a sacred gift is, to me, unimaginable. There's no greater calling than motherhood!*

\* \* \*

The picture window laced with snow framed Mark and Kip's faces when we finally arrived at my parents' house. As Jerry waded through the snow to carry my wheelchair inside, I fixed my gaze on the deserted yellow house trailer with faded brown shutters next door. Snow was packed against the front door and the heat had been turned down for the past two months, which was just as well—there wouldn't be time for a visit.

But I envisioned a light from the kitchen window and a silver foil tree on the bar with little-boy treasures tucked under it. Duke Dog, Lassie, and Pooh were waiting on top of the green safari bedspread with tigers in Kip's room. Or did they take Pooh to Ann's house? Kip didn't usually spend the night away from home without Pooh.

I figured the occasional invasion of a mouse or two was stilled in their search for a warmer dwelling. But oh, how I longed to warm our home with family tradition! To salve my heart with the simplicity it was sick for. I hoped our reunion, whenever it came, would bring with it a better sense of gratitude for the little things.

Grasping the two metal bars on my brace, I pulled with the strength I had in my hands, allowing the cold air that swept in when Jerry opened the truck door to filter between my chafed chin and the hard leather chin rest. Like scratching a mosquito bite, it was a temporary fix.

I could see my breath, and it felt good to drink in the cool, raw air. Jerry scooped me into his arms and we rushed like newlyweds toward the threshold of what many spinal-injury victims never get: a second chance. Entering my parents' house in a wheelchair seemed like a bad dream. I had to keep reminding myself that this would not be permanent, and how fortunate I was to even be there.

Pressed for time, Jerry pushed me to the bar where Mama had set a place for me. Daddy's blessing thanked God for more than the food and gifts. Christmas would be different, but the family was still intact.

After dinner, Mark and Kip opened my gifts for me. Some neighbors had given Mama money to buy me clothing, because many of my casual clothes before the accident were now too big. Jerry had done our shopping, mostly gift certificates. Santa would be bringing Kip the go-cart he wanted. I wouldn't be there to see his reaction, but just knowing we were able to get him something he'd especially wanted made me feel good. The plans were for him to spend the night there and, of course, Santa was instructed as to where he'd be on Christmas morning.

Daddy, who rarely shopped on his own, presented Mama and me with tiny diamond earrings. Mama had shopped for outfits for me to give Jerry—he was going to church now and needed them. I also had Clyde purchase a *Thompson Chain Reference Bible* for Jerry. We enjoyed watching the boys open their gifts, and then Jerry surprised me with a dainty solitary diamond necklace. It went perfectly with the earrings Daddy had given me.

After we finished exchanging presents, Jerry informed me it was time for catheterization. His first unsupervised attempt went smoothly. He measured and charted my urine output as instructed, and then redressed me. I was tempted to call him Dr. Miller, but kissing a doctor after a medical procedure just didn't feel right.

The black sky was still pelting the earth with layers of white when we headed back. We would miss the three-hour curfew allotted for our date, but it was Christmas—what could they say? The fact that my first time out under diverse circumstances was uneventful, and that Jerry proved himself capable of attending to my needs, awarded me weekend passes from then on.

When I was finally able to make short trips with Jerry to our "real" home, what I'd left behind on the morning of the accident had a different face. I was still the wife, the mother, the woman of the house, but under different pretenses. The refrigerator was keeping the leftover staples from spoiling, but there was no sign of a cook. The cabinets were barren of anything edible, and four straight-back chairs sat around a table that invited no one to feast. Nothing smelled of home, like chocolate or coffee or hairspray or life. The sound of high-heels clipping across linoleum was replaced by the haunting sound of a chair that rolled. My visits with Kip were generally somewhere else, and the most haunting sound of all was the stillness that had replaced the sound of a child at play.

But as I ponder an epilogue to the saga of my first trip home after the wreck, I think Christmas was enhanced by the Lord's generosity: he dumped enough white on us that we'd be hard-pressed to call it a blue Christmas!

\*    \*    \*

*In the natural, the trip seemed dangerous. And if they'd shared the idea with others, they would have most likely been advised to postpone the trip. You see, the wife was expecting their first child, a boy, and there were forces lurking against them. The husband was burdened with the responsibility of getting his fragile wife safely to their destination. But they pressed on in spite of the elements.*

*I wonder if they unknowingly passed by the tree that would eventually be used to hew out a cross that would not only change their lives, but the lives of humanity from henceforth. The tree that would scar the very one for which the journey was divinely orchestrated to protect. How could they know that their adventure would change the calendar and chart the course of time?*

*No doubt this husband was a bundle of nerves, as he knew he would have to attend to his wife's needs when the time came for the child to be born. But they chose to yield to the voice leading them, rather than their own reasoning, and followed the star to the place where Christmas began. And because they did, we can all meet the challenges set before us with hope. We can be overcomers in this world and residents of a mansion in the next one. Hallelujah, praise the Lamb!*

# 12

## GETTING UP TIME

*To everything there is a season, and a time to every purpose under heaven.*
—ECCLESIASTES 3:1

THERE WAS A MOVING in the water of my soul to stand up like one might get the urge to sing in an operatic pitch at the top of your lungs. It doesn't have to have rhyme or reason; you just feel like it, that's all. But Debbie said it was too early for me to try to stand, and I guess a physical therapist should know. Still, I had this reckless impulse that kept goading me, telling me that I just might be able to do it with some help. Why does everything have to be determined by some scientific calculation, anyway? *Every case is different*, I told myself. So I concocted a little plan.

I waited until a certain nursing assistant was on duty. She was the type who would throw caution to the wind. "I wonder what'd happen if I try to stand?" I asked Cassie one evening when she came in, as she routinely did, to shoot the bull.

She shrugged her shoulders. "I don't know. You wanna try?"

Did I want to try.

"Well, what could it hurt?" I responded, with cunning innocence.

I really didn't expect her to give me a professional answer, but I did think that if there was any real danger in standing a quadriplegic to her feet, Cassie should have been told.

"Well, let's try it," she said, like a kid joining a new club.

Cassie was accustomed to grabbing me under the armpits from behind my wheelchair to "boost" me (lift my derriere off my cushioned chair periodically to keep me from getting pressure spots). A boost Cassie was trained for; standing a paralyzed person to her feet, she was not. Nevertheless, she sprawled her legs out in front of my chair and before I could say scat she grabbed me under my arms and thrust me to my feet.

When my legs collapsed under me like a newborn fawn, Cassie caught me before I hit the floor and threw me back into the wheelchair. We gazed at each other in silence, equally shocked at what had just taken place. I realized then that my yearning didn't have a leg to stand on.

The next day I decided to tell Debbie what Cassie and I did. Her neck turned pink before she let me have it. "You did what? Don't you realize you could have been set back for weeks! This girl could lose her job over this." I had never seen Debbie that tenacious. She made me promise not to attempt anything so stupid ever again. And luckily, Dr. Martinat didn't get a whiff of it.

Still, the passion to stand impelled me. Physical therapy became a job I got up and went to every morning. My paycheck was when Debbie would flip her long dark hair behind her ears, smile shyly, and say, "Good!" She never said it as a mere compliment, like one might praise a child; if she said it, something new and positive had taken place. Days would pass between accolades. Some days the strain seemed like pulling an endless chain and all I wanted to do was get back into bed. But on those rare days when progress manifested, a second wind seemed to blow and strengthen me for another day of push and pull.

Maybe it was the performer within me, the need for someone to acknowledge my progress and pat me on the back. Or maybe I was just so stubborn that I wanted to prove I could do what they thought I couldn't. Probably all of the above. But my face was set like a flint toward the first step in the process of walking: standing up.

There were times when I'd get indignant toward something someone said or implied, especially if they were trying to let me down easy, as if I were expecting too much. Those incidents worked for my good, gave me an adrenaline rush. "You do better when you're mad," Debbie informed me.

Sometime after the botched attempt to stand prematurely, another nursing assistant with (I'm sorry) straw between her ears was the tour guide for a group of students. Before she filed them into my room, she lowered her voice and instructed them, "Don't ever tell a 'quad' they'll never walk again." The implication behind her comment was conde-scending: Don't tell a quad they'll never walk again, even though you know they won't.

But she forgot that I could hear a snail crawl. With eyes filled with fury and fueled to slap her hard with words, I shot back as her little convoy entered my observation chamber. "Don't tell a 'quad' they'll never walk again, because you don't *know* that!"

"Uh...yeah, that's right," the red-faced aide responded, as if she really believed it. I'm sure she never made that comment again, at least not within a hundred feet of a "quad."

I hated how the abbreviated form of the word quadriplegic rolled from insensitive tongues, stigmatizing those who experienced paraly-sis in all four limbs. To me it implied finality, a perpetual cope-don't-hope mindset. Call it what you want: stubborn, rude, or denial. I don't care. I call it survival! It doesn't seem unreasonable to me to believe that the God who enabled Abraham to sport a snaggle-toothed grin when Sarah's belly started protruding at age ninety can return strength to arms and legs at any stage of one's life!

God didn't give me a strong personality without reason. I believe he knew I'd need it. For me, being upright was a "Hobson's choice." Thomas Hobson was a stable keeper in Cambridge, England during the 1600s who stubbornly rented the horse nearest his stable door or none at all. It sounds like he was just ornery, which solidifies that I may very well be a direct descendent of this Thomas Hobson. Oddly, or maybe not, my grandpa's name was Thomas Leo Hobson and my dad's given name is John Thomas Hobson.

I was determined to stand on my wobbly legs eventually. If they crumbled, they crumbled. If I had to fight this ugly war with a body deadened from the neck down to everything but pain, I'd fight it. There were unseen forces on my side; I had no doubt about that. And aren't we all warriors in some kind of earthly battle? On weak days when there was no fight left, and there were many, I coasted. But I'm confident that God's hand never left mine.

If I had understood about the authority of the believer, spiritual warfare, and the weapons available through Jesus' blood, his name, and his word, it would have given me an edge. But thank God, he knows the level we are on spiritually and deals with us accordingly. I find it sad that many denominational churches stop with the message of salvation. It's like a child who mopes through his father's house hungry, broke, and unclothed while his food sits untouched on the table, his allowance is tucked in his billfold, and his clothes are hanging in the closet. But the child walks around deprived and thinking it's enough just to bear his father's name.

I may not have understood my rightful position in Christ, but he came to where I was and gave me a fighting spirit. For that I'm thankful. And I did know this: What once was dead was coming to life, and I had to give it my best shot.

✻   ✻   ✻

I pressed toward the day when, with Debbie's supervision, I would attempt a walk between the parallel bars. Neither of us knew what to expect, but when Debbie said it was time, my heart did a summersault. Thank God for second chances! As humans we often get impatient and attempt to reach our goals before we're really prepared. It takes training to develop physical, intellectual, and spiritual muscles. Learning to discern God's timing and then having the patience to wait takes spiritual growth and character.

Debbie came to pick me up herself on the morning of my trial walk. "Are you ready for this?" she asked, smiling with anticipation for the goal she, too, had worked hard for.

"You know I am!" I answered, nervously.

As she pushed my chair along, Debbie warned me not to expect too much on my first effort. The memory of my legs crumbling on my first, unauthorized attempt to stand lingered too strong for my mind to allow me to be disappointed if I didn't have a stellar performance. Anything positive would work.

When we arrived on the basement level of the building where the Physical Therapy Department was located, we were greeted by three spectators for the event: Daddy, who left work to come over to watch me walk, Mama, and my new friend, Alvin Stevens.

Alvin was a fourth floor patient whose outrageous smile had captured my attention in therapy weeks before I got the nerve to speak to him. His charisma had the drawing power of a red-tag sale. He'd been a quadriplegic for several years after an automobile accident and was in for therapy. You didn't have to talk to Alvin long to learn that the Lord was the source of his joy. We clicked immediately. And once you got to know him, all you saw was his face: handsome and full of God.

Alvin's presence with my parents at the end of my tiny runway spoke volumes about the man. There wasn't a selfish bone in his body. He was elated that there was a possibility that I might walk again. And he was as concerned about Jerry's needs as he was mine. Only God could instill that kind of spirit into a man. His being there was the prelude to my song and dance.

Debbie asked Bonnie, another therapist, to aid her in lifting me from my chair. Bonnie secured my left side, while Debbie held me on my right side and called the shots.

"Okay, ready?"

"Ready," I said, and the two women hoisted me to my feet.

I couldn't stand alone, but miraculously my legs didn't crumble.

With her free hand, Debbie forced my right fist to open and grasp the bar. She instructed Bonnie to do the same with my left hand. It taxed my concentration for me to keep both hands holding to the bars while trying to balance. The therapists kept a tight grip.

Debbie felt the struggle going on inside me. "Okay, just relax... we've got you. Now, try to slide your right foot forward." She knew picking it up was too much to ask.

Debbie and Bonnie weren't nearly as tall as I'd thought, and if I'd been able to stand with good posture, I'd probably have met them eye-to-eye. The weight of my body sent a surge of pain through my posterior. My rump wanted to sink. And the three hopefuls at the other end of the bars now seemed miles away. But I couldn't let my encouraging trio down. I reached into the pit of my insides and drew out enough strength to shift my right foot forward.

"Great!" Debbie shouted. "Now do the left foot...come on!"

I shifted my weight to my right side and then slid my left foot forward. It felt like lead. I heard Mama sniffle, but I dared not risk losing focus by looking up.

"You're doing great!" Debbie applauded me. "Let's make one more step while you're at it."

I repeated the regiment just before my legs began dancing with spasms so violent that Debbie and Bonnie were also shaking. Debbie reached for my chair with her foot and they lowered me. Although I made only two feeble steps, they were steps. And we learned that my legs could hold me up once I regained balance—it was the spasms that forced me down.

When my parents watched me take my first steps at nine months old, I'm sure they never fathomed that they'd be cheering me on to take a step twenty-five years later. Mama and Grandma Davis have told stories about me jumping like a monkey in my crib. According to them, I had an early eagerness to roam. The newness and excitement of learning to walk is a normal process that none of us remembers. Relearning it is not, and I'll never forget the experience.

There was no hoopla, no newsperson or cameraman; it was a private affair. But heart flags were being waved from a small gathering in adoration to the King of kings and Lord of lords. Debbie beamed with pride at the results of months of hard work. My parents' were teary-eyed. And, as usual, Alvin radiated a joyful smile. I don't consider it cocky to think that at least one angel was clapping. I know Jesus was.

I returned to my room more exhausted than I used to be after roving full court for an entire basketball game. As I lay resting, I summoned God: "Thank you for the two steps today. But if I'm going to *really* walk, you'll have to stop the shaking."

Nothing seems to happen quickly with me. But as my steps increased, the violent spasms decreased. Praise God!

A dark-haired lady in her mid-thirties, with a creamy complexion and perfect features who I just remember as Virginia, introduced me to Philippians 4:13: *I can do all things through Christ which strengtheneth me.* A freak accident where a horse jumped onto the car she was riding in had left her a quadriplegic. Her reference to that verse when she couldn't even lift a finger moved me. I recall picking her hand up and moving it for her once in the day room. The dead weight was heavy and I struggled to lift it, but I felt a sense of satisfaction that I was able to do even such a small thing for her.

After that, I wanted Philippians 4:13 visible at all times in my room, so I could be encouraged by it and the jewel of a woman who had introduced me to it. I had Jerry bring me some construction paper and a large magic marker. Each night he would prop me up in bed before he left and place the red sheet of construction paper and marker on my food tray. Holding the pen taxed muscles that had surrendered to injury and ignited excruciating pain across my upper back and shoulders. It took me one week to write that verse of scripture, but when Jerry taped it to my window, it became an inspiring piece of art. Not because of its beauty—it was extremely primitive—but because of its context. Philippians 4:13 became mine from then on, and it did not go unnoticed.

"You don't actually believe that do you?" an oversized male nurse commented one day when he brought my dinner tray in.

"I sure do!" I answered.

He didn't give me a chance to elaborate. He just shook his head as he left. I'm sure he viewed my beliefs as a cop out, (after all, many seem to get "religion" after they're reduced to nothing). I believed that verse, but he'd never let me explain why. I believed it like I believed my brace was crafted in hell and he needed to lose a hundred pounds. I believed it because Virginia was living proof of it. I believed it because God confirms his word to my heart through the Holy Spirit. And whether he liked it or not, that male nurse had to see it every time he walked into my room.

*       *       *

Timing through God's eyes is much different from ours. But how crucial it is to move at the proper time. My standing-up day came in his time, not mine. And I didn't let the spasms shake my faith. Down the road, religion nearly did. But thankfully, God has sent enlightenment through the revelation of his word and various teachers. Not everyone can see me totally healed with eyes of faith. And that's okay. Some days it's hard for me, too. But God was gracious to send me Alvin and Virginia for reinforcement when the waiting was hard. And I'm grateful for my strong Catholic therapist, Debbie, who pushed me to try a little harder. And no doubt, he sent the doubters by my path, also. And when I get weary from the struggle (seemingly every other day), I have to stop and remember that a thousand years to God is like a day, and that *he which hath begun a good work in you* (in me) *will perform it until the day of Jesus Christ* (Philippians 1:6). Even if it kills him. Come to think of it, it did. About two days ago.

# 13

## THE LOVE CHAPTER

*By night on my bed I sought him whom my soul loveth: I sought him, but I found him not.* —THE SONG OF SOLOMON 3:1

THE BRIDE OF SOLOMON 3:1 is describing the yearning she has for her mate. Many things can happen to dull that yearning, I guess, but paralysis isn't one of them. So far, I could not feel from the neck down, which proves an important point: Love is in the heart; libido is in the head.

Word leaked out at John C. Whitaker Rehabilitation Center about a motel-like room where patients were allowed to go and spend the night, or even a weekend, with their mates. Even though I was allowed short trips home on Saturdays and Sundays, Jerry and I had not spent a night alone together. Encaged in a brace and leashed to a catheter didn't set an idealistic stage for romance, but I longed to simply lie undisturbed in my husband's arms. To feel his breath and smell his skin. To close my eyes and escape in his kisses.

I was perturbed at Dr. Martinat, because I had to hear everything through the rehabilitative grapevine. If something good was available, I thought he ought to make me aware of it. Seniority had awarded me a certain amount of clout when it came to gossip among nurses and patients, but up until now my energy had not been focused on intimacy (to a physical degree) with Jerry.

"So, what's this ADL Room everybody's talking about?" I finally quizzed him.

He flashed me one of his fatherly looks. Time pulled at the center won me no brownie points with him. "You're not ready for that," he snapped, and then started to walk away.

Talk about déjà vu!

"Hey, why not?" I demanded.

He turned around and then reached to tighten the screws on my brace, like he always did when he wanted to shut me up. For some reason, I'm reminded now of how Mama made me wear wool trousers under my pretty dresses on really cold days in the first grade. The wool pants scratched my legs and made me look silly, but she thought warm legs took precedence over looks. Dr. Martinat was more concerned about my overall well being than immediate gratification. But I felt as though I had lost more than my mobility and the skills that went it. Somewhere in this condescending process, I'd lost the freedom to make my own choices. I felt like I was in the first grade again.

I confess there were incidences when I acted like a child. Once when Dr. Martinat did his tighten-Sandra's-chin-brace thing when Mama was with me in PT, I deliberately scratched him on the hand! At that point, my mother questioned if I had really dropped from her womb. But sometimes you give up and yield to your inner child. It certainly doesn't help matters, of course, but it makes you feel better at the time.

"Why can't Jerry and I spend the night together in that room?" I insisted.

"I'll let you know when you're ready," he informed me. What did he think we would do in there, swing from the chandelier? He knew me well enough by now to figure I'd rub his skin on that same spot until it festered. So, the next day a thirty-something, executive-looking guy tapped lightly on my door before stepping in.

"Mrs. Miller?"

"Yes?"

"Hi, I'm Doug Smith, uh…I understand you were inquiring about the ADL (Activities for Daily Living) Room for you and your husband." And then he presented me with this book about sex for quads. Even though I was walking with aid, I was again snared with that prefix and its limitations. I could feel my cheeks getting hot as he flipped the pages filled with explicit pictures in front of me. I could only image the description on the insurance claim for this one.

"Dr. Martinat is very timid when it comes to things of this nature," Doug explained. I considered the paradox of Dr. Martinat popping the elastic on my underpants first thing every morning with an investigative eye. Doug broke my thoughts. "Do you have any questions?"

I wanted to ask him what his job title was, but I didn't want to detain his exit, so I shook my head. He laid his business card on top of the "sexualia" left on the nightstand. "Well, if you think of anything, just have a nurse give me a call and I'll come back and talk to you some more."

*Fat chance of that,* I thought, as he turned to leave. "Oh yeah," he wheeled around, "don't mention the book to Dr. Martinat."

That night the second-shift nurses congregated in my room and gawked over the picture book like junior high students at a pajama party. I finally told them just to take the thing to the nursing station. I felt uneasy with it laying next to my Bible, anyhow. I never understood the necessity of that little visit from Doug, or his book, but I took his advice and never mentioned it to Dr. Martinat.

\* \* \*

Sometimes I wonder why certain incidences hang age-stained in my memory's file while others slip away with the first breeze that passes. I'm glad this one stuck, if for nothing else but the pure hilarity of it. Due to the nature of the following sequences, please allow for surrogate wording.

What can I say? The natural hunger for love (expressed) was gnawing a hole in the pit of our starving…whatever it is that love gnaws at. Our stomachs were protruding and malnutrition was about to set in. Jerry and I were past substitutional hormonal gratification. Way past. The next step was rickets of the, oh, let's call it LOVENOID—Love Now Or I'll Die!

Love truly is blind. I'm starry-eyed and greasy-headed, poured into an unsightly brace from my chin to my navel, which is beginning to sour—the chin rest on the brace, that is—and my water drainage tube is in close proximity to…well, you know, and Jerry doesn't even care that I resemble ET.

By now we both felt close enough to Cindi Allen to pass a couple of hints about our situational state of minds. Cindi was sympathetic, even volunteered to assist. By assist I mean instruct us as to what not to bother, etc. In essence, she said it wouldn't hurt to go fishing while draining the pond. (Maybe this memory should remain silent.) But it wouldn't be fair to drop you now. Please pray that my daddy doesn't read this, though.

After our intimate chat, Cindi admonished us to enjoy each other, turned the light out, and then hung a NO VISITORS sign on the door. We couldn't help but wonder if we would be quizzed at the end of this little rendezvous so she could document the outcome for some hospital study. Thoughts like that, and the possibility of someone ignoring the sign on the door, can really alter romantic intentions. Anyway, with all the to-do about it, we felt obligated, so Jerry undressed down to his shorts and crawled into the tiny bed with me.

"Who needs that old room?" he softly whispered, as he snuggled his good-smelling self next to the brace that encaged me. Now Jerry and I both have ample lips, but I've got to tell you, puckering past that mess was challenging. We decided we needed just to relax and cozy up to each other, so we took a few deep breaths and tried to get used to the fact that we were actually lying side by side in spite of the contraption between us. Then Jerry carelessly hit his head over the red ball dangling above us and a high-pitched voice thundered, "Can I help you?" Funny. It rarely worked when I actually needed somebody.

"Accident," I responded. "Now, where were we?"

"Right here," Jerry mused, forming another long pucker.

And then it happened: tap, tap, tap at the door. How could Cindi have let someone by?

"Pretend you're asleep," Jerry instructed, as he freed himself from the brace that had imprinted itself on his chest and leaped into his pants like a long-legged frog.

"But, what if…"

"Never mind, just do it," he whispered, on his way to the door.

It was my cousin Claudia Porter.

\*  \*  \*

*Claudia was my "city cousin" who came to the country in the summer when we were kids to get away from paved streets, buses, and the smokestacks from the RJ Reynolds Archer plant behind their house on Reich Street. She was the cousin I loved to spend a week with in the summer, because I was awed at the paved streets with tiny houses lined up like piano keys. Some of the houses on the rural dirt road where I lived were as far apart as the entire length of Reich Street. The thrill derived from the dinging bell of the ice cream truck approaching on a steamy summer afternoon was like being in a storybook; an ice-cold Brown Mule or orange Popsicle was tastier when delivered by a man in an ice cream truck. And you could actually walk to the grocery store from Claudia's house on Reich Street.*

*Lying on a quilt in her backyard in our bathing suits with a romance magazine and a transistor radio would never happen at my house, which made it that much more intriguing. And boys we liked were just a skip and a hop away. The time her mom caught us smoking on the side porch only got us a good scolding; if we'd got caught smoking at my house, I wouldn't have sat down for a month!*

*But then Claudia didn't have horses at her disposal and golden fields that touched the sky. Speaking to strangers was considered a courtesy in our neck of the woods. And everyone knew each other at the country church. Chasing lightning bugs and hand-cranked ice cream were summer afternoon delights. And party-line eavesdropping was one way we got our kicks.*

*Claudia and I lived very different lives, with her being from the twin city—Winston-Salem—and me being from Yadkin County, better described as "the country"; but we each enjoyed the diversity from her house to mine. And we shared the same grandparents, with Uncle Bill— her daddy—being Mama's brother. I remember summer nights spent at our grandparents' farm and Grandma Davis preparing a steaming kettle to place by Claudia's bedside when her asthma would attack. When we were very young, her wheezing would awake me. But I'd go right back to sleep, never really comprehending her struggle. And coming from a family of five children, she learned better than I the grace of sharing.*

*Claudia was with Mama and me on the memorable night that I won a colt at a horseshow. Mama gave both of us a dollar to buy a ticket. Right before the drawing, Claudia and I said a silent prayer. I always held my breath and blew my cheeks full of air when I had a serious request to God, like it would get his attention better. "I prayed I'd win that colt," I told Claudia.*

*"I prayed you'd win it, too," my cousin and friend replied. Looking back, I figure it was her prayer that caused the winning ticket to be mine.*

*A memorable element of our relationship was the untamed giggling that erupted when we were together. We had this special handshake routine we'd invented as kids, and we still did it after we were grown. Kind of like a secret club thing that bonded us. And it always ignited giggling.*

*I say giggling, because giggling is different from laughter. Anybody can laugh. But it takes a special connection between two people for the kind of giggling to erupt that you can't control even if you know one more giggle will kill you.*

\* \* \*

So when I heard Jerry lie, "Hey Claudia. Um, Sandra's asleep," I knew my work was cut out for me. Claudia is enough like my mom that she is not easily dissuaded. "I'll just sit here until she wakes up," she replied, ducking under Jerry's arm to enter the dark room.

The two of them sat whispering courtesies across my body for an extremely boring amount of time. "How's Kip?" "Fine." "How about George?" "Fine." And on and on they chatted, as if whispers across the body wouldn't stir a person like me. Finally, I could no longer hold the laugh bubbles backing up in my lungs. The combustion crept up my throat and out between my tightened lips like a deflating balloon. Claudia jolted, and then joined right in when I opened my eyes and let rolls of giggles relieve me.

"You scared me half to death!" she scolded me, before piecing the puzzle together. Jerry didn't stand a chance, so we confessed to a conspiracy and the picture of the whole scenario did us all good.

Someone once described laughter as "a tranquilizer with no side effects." But I dare to differ in this instrance—my sides were aching by the time Claudia left. And by then, of course, visiting hours and "the mood" were over. I guess it was just as well, because Dr. Martinat was right: Jerry and I weren't ready to share sleeping quarters. I feared hurting him with all my gadgets as much as he feared hurting me with his passion. Besides, real love can wait until the right season. In our case, we'd already endured nearly two seasons. And spring was just around the corner.

\* \* \*

A few weeks later I got to visit the apartment reserved for lovers, but not for a rendezvous with my husband. Instead it was to perform an assignment for occupational therapy. I had to bake something.

The real life challenges that I faced had to be tested before my discharge, but I was not mentally ready for some of them. Setting myself up for failure wasn't comfortable. But life outside was waiting for my reentrance, so I had to be pushed out of the nest. Menial tasks like pouring milk into a bowl, holding a toothbrush, and getting dressed had still not been accomplished. But to be scrutinized while struggling with such mindless tasks punctured my ego. Nevertheless, I gritted my teeth, determined to pass every test necessary to equip myself for life at home.

"What would you like to bake?" asked Mary, who hailed from the Occupational Therapy Department. She was older than my usual OT therapist, Gail. I envisioned Mary as a tennis player with two teenage boys named Dru and Shay, although she never said. You know the type: a wide gold wedding band, dark hair in a mid-length undercut, lips the color of the inside part of a peach that's closest to the seed. Her black-rimmed glasses were attached to a gold chain and laid on her freshly pressed white blouse for easy pick-up.

"Well, I might could bake one of those cup-of-this-cup-of-that cobblers," I answered, while allowing my eyes to roam the apartment from my wheelchair.

"Okay," Mary said. "What all will you need?" She started peeking into the cabinets.

"Flour and sugar."

"Hmm…" she mumbled, stretching to retrieve a sack of half-used Dixie Crystal sugar from the cabinet. She reached for the small bag of Martha White flour, which had also been opened and asked, "Is self-rising flour what you need?"

"Yep. And oh, I'll need some milk and margarine, too."

Mary opened the unsmudged refrigerator door and revealed a few staples: a three-liter Pepsi, a pack of American cheese, mustard, a jar of strawberry jam, Mrs. Filbert's margarine, and a carton of milk. She set the milk and a stick of margarine on the round oak table in the center of the kitchen, and then wheeled me to it. "Here we go," she said. "Now, what else do you need?"

"Some kind of fruit," I replied.

Mary searched the nearly barren cabinets for a can of fruit, but could only come up with some sliced pineapple. I'd never heard of a pineapple cobbler, but I wanted to get this over with. "Well, why not?" I asked.

Mary seemed to understand my anxiousness. "I'm game if you are." She searched the cabinets for what I'd need to work with: a measuring cup, a glass mixing bowl, a wooden spoon, and a rectangular Pyrex dish. "Okay," Mary started explaining, "I want you to do everything you can, but if you can't do something, I'll help you."

That feeling you get when tears are forming on the other side of your eyes likes clouds holding back a thunder burst threatened me. I was sure, as I forced the wooden spoon between my fingers on my right hand and struggled to spoon a cup of flour out of the bag and into the measuring cup, that if I blinked my eyes would rain tears and I'd flunk the test. Somehow I managed not to cry and got the dry ingredients successfully into the mixing bowl. Mary added the milk.

"Oh, I forgot; we need to turn on the oven and melt the margarine in the Pyrex dish," I inserted. Mary loosened the paper from the margarine and handed it to me. I dumped it, paper and all, into the Pyrex dish. Mary never said a word; she just reached into the dish and removed the paper.

"What do we need to set the oven on?" she asked.

I assumed this therapist had done this before—the step-by-step instructions from me were part of the test. It was like taking Home Economics again without my girlfriends. Or my hands.

"Uh, three fifty will probably do." Mary set the dial and inserted the dish after the oven preheated.

I made a stab at stirring the ingredients in the bowl. After a few seconds, Mary removed the dish and melted margarine from the stove and placed it on a potholder on the table in front of me. " Be careful. I don't want you to burn yourself," she said.

I sat staring at the hot dish and the bowl of half mixed sugar, flour, and milk. "Is there another spoon I can dip this out with?" Mary rambled in the drawer where the utensils were kept and came out with a deeper metal spoon. I transferred the ingredients into the Pyrex dish one meticulous spoonful at a time. The rotary motion was wreaking havoc on my shoulders and neck, but determination kept me at it. I didn't want to have to repeat this test.

Mary turned the bowl up and scraped out what I couldn't, and then opened the can of pineapple slices with a can opener she found in a drawer. "Do you think you can use a fork with a built-up handle and get the pineapple out?" she asked.

"Yes," I said, but I didn't know.

Mary forced the big-handled fork to slide between my fisted fingers on my right hand, and I slowly forked each slice out of the can and pitched them into the dish like throwing catfish in a bucket. At least none of them slithered away. Then I arranged the slices side by side in the chalky, white batter. Mary looked at her watch. "How long will it take to cook?" she asked, while placing the dish in the oven.

"Probably about thirty minutes," I said, but it only took twenty. The dough rose around the pineapple slices like peddles on a daisy. The smell had us both drooling—we devoured my whole project!

I vetoed Mary's suggestion that I try to wash the dishes from my wheelchair. The thought of sitting to perform this everyday task gave me an adrenaline rush. I started pushing myself up from the wheelchair. "What are you doing?" asked a ruffled Mary. "Are you going to stand? You don't have to stand up."

"Yeah, I do!" I retorted. She grabbed my arm to steady me, and I leaned against the sink and whisked those dishes through the suds in the sink of water Mary had made. She guarded me like a hen over her chick, and I was sure she'd rather I'd stayed securely put in the wheelchair. Her job was to teach me to work sitting down. But I couldn't accept that convenience. A mountain was trying—ever so slowly—to move, and I didn't want to stop it.

*   *   *

*My beloved spake, and said unto me, Rise up, my love, my fair one, and come away. For, lo, the winter is past, the rain is over and gone* (The Song of Solomon 2:10–11).

Jerry appeared on the night allotted for our romantic retreat in the ADL Room with an overnight bag and the arms I so desperately needed to sink into without interruption. Cindi Allen had drilled him on the when and what's of my numerous medications and who to call if a situation arose. But this man knew me like no other. I was confident Jerry could solve any problems we'd face. I had been weaned from the catheter, and could use the toilet with assistance. It wasn't the best of situations, but it was a far cry from where I'd been.

My weekly shower consisted of being hosed down, brace and all, while lying on a gurney in a specially built shower stall. The nurses hated giving patients showers, because they always came out wet, too. But I itched—in the places where I could feel—like a puppy with fleas. One happy night, I talked a second-shift nurse into sliding my brace off long enough to give my scalp a good scrubbing. I would have given her a hundred-dollar bill if she'd done that all night. Unfortunately, that treat ended when the omniscient Dr. Martinat found out about it. I got the weekly showers, but no more removing the brace.

So when Jerry scooped me up, wearing nothing but a brace, and lowered me into a real bathtub filled with tingly bubbles, it was like emerging into a fountain of bliss. There was only one problem: my legs kept floating to the top of the water. And should I have accidentally slipped and my head went under, I'd have drowned right then and there in that MARVELOUS room!

The obvious sacrifices Jerry made for me to enjoy a little normalcy cut my heart to the core. But he never seemed agitated. He lifted my dripping-wet body from the water and patted every inch of me dry like a lover instead of a caregiver, and that made all the difference, all the difference in the world.

Jerry carried me to a real chair at the same table where I'd made the pineapple cobbler a few weeks prior, and we had a quiet dinner that he'd brought from a restaurant. And then my husband took my hands and lifted me to my feet. His hands were strong and trusting. "Walk to me," he said, and then turned me loose.

Panic crept up my spine. "No," I cried, reaching for him. "I'll fall!"

Jerry was determined to force a solo step from me. "I won't let you fall." I knew he wouldn't, but my legs wobbled in retreat. "Sandra, walk to me."

So I did.

An "activity for daily living" forced from me by the same one who motivated me to move my big toe on my left foot in the hospital months earlier. The one whose arms I buried my soul in until the breaking of a new day. No hospital noise. No blasting intercoms in the middle of the night. Just the beat of my lover's heart pulsating against my ear. And a knowing inside that, no matter what, love never fails.

# 14

## HOME FIRES BURNING

*If I ascend into heaven, thou art there; if I make my bed in hell, behold, thou art there.* —PSALMS 139:8

I WAS NO TALLER THAN a dandelion when someone let Pretty Boy out of his cage. I'd had the teeny yellow and green parakeet long enough that he was a definite member of our family. Every time he managed an escape, though, he was like a convict who'd just finagled his way out of the slammer. For reasons unknown, he usually ended up lighting on my head, and then Mama would bend over laughing when he'd leave a deposit and she'd have to take a bath cloth to my scalp. Mama always found more humor in that than I did. I was more concerned with Pretty Boy's safety—he just couldn't understand that the little house of wire swinging over the lamp with the red shade in the corner of our living room was his protection from predators who'd love to scoop him up for dinner. So you can imagine the fit I cut the day he got free and flew out the front door. I was sure Pretty Boy was a goner!

As usual, my hero came through. Daddy climbed up in the big oak tree, just beyond where our yard stopped, and rescued the poor little bird from the woes of freedom. Pretty Boy came out frightened but unscathed, which is more than I can say for Daddy; he took a free-fall with Pretty Boy in hand and sprained his ankle. Things that caused me so much distress seemed hilarious to Mama, but then, she's not a very serious person. Come to think of it, Pretty Boy eventually met his maker after she went on a cleaning frenzy and sprayed him and his wire cage with cologne. She has this thing with cologne.

I think I know how Pretty Boy felt when the fresh air of the outside world hit him in the face, though. The day that Dr. Martinat released me from that tormenting brace, I felt like I'd peeled off a thousand miseries.

"Do you want to keep your brace?" he asked.

"No, thank you!" I replied. "I never want to see it again!"

"Well, do you mind if we keep it for someone who might need it, but doesn't have insurance?"

"By all means," I told him, but my heart wrenched for the poor soul who might inherit that anguish.

The week prior to my March 15, 1976 departure date was busied with visits from various specialists offering advice on how to cope in a world much different that I'd known. I took their advice in stride, but with a strong spirit-sense that the three-legged cane I now walked with was a temporary aid. Debbie had been the physical therapist who had worked with me the longest, so it seemed only fitting that she be the one Dr. Martinat would send to East Bend to scout out potential dangers of my being home alone. After careful examination of our little nest, Debbie concluded that things were not accessible enough for me to be safe unsupervised while Jerry and Kip were away at work and school. But Debbie had worked with me long enough to know that her report was one thing; what I'd do was another.

My brief chat with the psychologist before departure was unfruitful. At that point, I refused to admit to myself, let alone another, that my head had become a brewery where evil potions were being stirred. The circumstances that brought unnatural fears were foreign and not of my choosing. I assumed these awful feelings of panic were an aftermath of the trauma of the injury, and that they would dissipate when normal life resumed. Pushing it under the rug was a performance I repeated, but it became harder and harder to play that role. Eventually I would have no choice but acknowledge that my mind and emotions had become a danger zone. I was spiritually anemic in regard to the supernatural world, so I let my mind marinate in the lethal juices of fear, thinking that a "real" Christian wouldn't need a doctor who dealt with "tricks of the mind."

A dietitian made her visit with suggestions for a high-calorie diet to help me put some meat on my tailbone. At ninety-two pounds, it literally hurt to sit in a chair for very long. She suggested I drink a lot of milkshakes. I received that as a word of wisdom, and even though I am way past being bothered with my tailbone lacking enough padding to sit comfortably in a chair, milkshakes (and also ice cream) still seem like a good remedy for a lot that ails me.

To sum up my departure rundown, another face appeared prior to Jerry's arrival to pick me up. Remember the nurse in the Emergency Room who came in after the accident with a soft collar and told me I could go home? Well, this lady's job was to present me with another one to wear home.

"You'll need to wear this for precaution every time you ride in a car," she announced.

"You've got to be kidding," I retorted.

"I'm afraid I'm not."

"Now let me get this straight. You're saying that I've got to wear this collar around my neck every time I ride in an automobile?"

"Well, I highly recommend it."

"From now on?"

"Oh yes, for the rest of your life. You don't want to risk another neck injury."

Need I even bother to paint a picture of that collar in a box marked *Goodwill?* I may have carried war scars home, but this wounded bird was free. Free to let the summer wind blow in my face on amusement rides at Myrtle Beach. Free to lock-in four-wheel drive and explore wild terrain with Jerry on hunting trails in the mountains. I'm telling you, I was free, and come what may, I intended to stay free!

Jerry came in Ole Silver for my discharge. His sister, Linda, brought her car to transport the rest of my accumulated belongings to our home. We stopped at the nursing station and said goodbye to many who had become more than caregivers. As days folded into weeks, my room had become a sounding board for personal problems and work frustrations. I recall a young nurse dashing into my room after having her feelings hurt by an inconsiderate doctor. She stayed there until we talked her tears dry. I was often ears to martial and boyfriend problems and eyes to admire pictures of kids and grandchildren. The goofy neighbors in one of Cassie's stories ended up being my kinfolks. Cindi was the oldest of a slew of siblings, married, and bossy—the perfect candidate for a head nurse. Georgia, head nurse on the day shift, was sweet and homegrown. Joy was single, naive, and energetic. Being from Yadkin County, Shelia and I had much in common. Debbie was dating the big male nurse, although with his attitude, I never understood why. I'm sure by now I've been lost with the memory of hundreds of other patients, but I still see them as they were nearly thirty years ago.

*   *   *

Lavender crocus peaked through tender blades of new grass and daffodils stretched toward the early spring sky like yellow teacups. And the spirit of resurrection filled my heart. Adversity had separated our threesome, but tonight we would rest together on home turf. I pushed—ever so slowly—the apple-red wheelchair, which Dr. Martinat had insisted I'd need, through the door that led to a world laden with barriers and obstacles to overcome. The protective shield of John C. Whitaker Rehabilitation Center had climaxed, but we would not be hiring a wife sitter. Freedom did not come without a price—I was as frightened as a first-day kindergartner. And I found that the weeks of training were a mere scratch on the surface of reality. Proving I could survive without constant surveillance was now my mission.

That night our extended family met at our home for a small celebration. Atop the purple cake that Ann brought was an edible horseshoe and the word WELCOME. The kids took turns riding in my wheelchair, but when Tony and Ann's eight-year-old son, Tim, asked if he could get one for Christmas, the well wishers decided it was time to leave.

And so there we were: a more mature Jerry, a very different Sandra, and a fragile Kip, who had to readjust. Nearly six months had past since Kip had moved in with Tony and Ann, and for a seven-year-old, that was a long span of his life. I was forced to face my greatest fear when I stepped into the bathroom while he was taking his bath. He flinched as if I were a stranger, hung his head, and said the words I prayed I'd never hear: "I'm used to Ann." I swallowed the lump that my son's truthfulness produced in my throat, reminded him to wash behind his ears, and stepped away. I'd have to ease back into my role as Mom in our home.

The menial tasks I so wanted to accomplish seemed unreachable. The first real housework I managed on my own was folding some bath cloths. With my limited range of motion and spasticity in my fingers, simple tasks were not only difficult, but painful as well. Every attempt, though, stretched me physically and spiritually. I learned that failure is only a forerunner to success, and patience is an added virtue in a lifelong marathon. I figure it's okay to throw up your hands to the things you simply can't change, as long as you do your best to work the kinks out of possibilities. Things like playing the piano, hot curling my hair, or sowing a button on a shirt ended up as "oh wells" that would have to wait. And staying upright on a gravitating earth was, and is, a never-ending challenge. Someone should shout "TIM–BER" as I'm going down, because I hit the ground, or floor, like a redwood in a windfall. Trust me, after several hard blows to the face and head, one begins to tiptoe lightly through the forest. But God must have given me a "hard head" literally, as well as metaphorically, because I've sprung back from some dillies!

At first I could not turn over in bed without Jerry's help. But it didn't take him long to figure out a system: he turned me every time he turned, whether I needed to or not. It soon became like a reflex. And every morning before he left for work, he'd pull me out of bed and lead me to the couch, placing my cane within reach. I'd call Kip about an hour before time for the school bus to arrive, and then talk him through fixing his breakfast (usually cereal). I made sure his clothes were laid out the night before. We made it fine, except for an occasional cowlick and tying his tennis shoes—for some reason he tied them backward, which meant they never stayed tied long. But Kip never had any trouble tying mine. I can see him as if it were yesterday, getting off the bus with Mark in the evening with his blonde hair tasseled, shoes untied, and jeans frayed around the bottom from being just a smidgen too long.

Kip adjusted better than I to our new lifestyles—kids seem to have a way of taking things as they come. And he learned, earlier than most, how to do a lot for himself. But he never stopped needing what I could offer—hugs, kisses, and words of love and admonition. You simply don't stop being a person of value because you can't physically perform some menial task.

I credit Kip's kitchen savvy from our giving him liberty to experiment with cooking at such an early age. He gets a little carried away with his "critter cuisine," though. And let the record be known that I am in no way responsible for his menus. I usually try, sometimes with reluctance, to taste everything he sticks in my face. That is, unless I suspect it might be something funky like raccoon, 'possum, or worse!

It's our neighbor, Bogie, who has been his prime guinea pig through the years. And it's usually "the best he's ever ate."

Living next door to my parents was a blessing in disguise. Mama came every day to help me bathe and get dressed. And most of the time, it was she who took me back for therapy three times a week. Neighbors chipped in and helped out when they could. Polly, a long-time friend and aunt by marriage, could think of things to do that wouldn't enter anybody else's mind. Once when we returned from a beach trip, we found our bedroom windows decked with new curtains. We just looked at each other and said, "Polly!"

At Ann's insistence, we had dinner at their house every Tuesday night for ever so long. I think she was so used to Jerry and Kip being there that she needed to see them at least once a week, which was fine with me. Ann's a great cook and we ate a lot of home-cooked meals at our mothers' houses. And we ate out at lot until I felt comfortable maneuvering around the kitchen. We feel very fortunate that each of Jerry's sisters, Ann, Linda, and Jeanette, has always been willing to do anything they could for us. And in spite of the fact that everybody knows everybody else's business, there's really nothing like small-town living. When things are rough, people really come through for you. The local Jaycees even sponsored a benefit for us, raising a thousand dollars, which we added to our savings for a down payment on a house. While in the hospital, money was donated from members of our high school senior class, various churches, and individuals. You simply can't repay that kind of graciousness and generosity.

Although I had adapted to using a spoon and fork with a built-up handle, at first I was a slight threat to those around me. Jerry found it easier to feed me when we ate at restaurants. I know I was overly sensitive, but some of the stares were difficult to swallow. Looking back, it probably wasn't as bad as I thought—it's just natural to glance at someone who's different. But pride still had the reigns. The thing that bothered me worse than being stared at was when I was deliberately ignored, not that we aren't all guilty at some point of being intimidated by someone with a noticeable handicap. But people would actually ask Jerry, or whomever I was with, a question about me when I was right in front of them! I'd generally make them feel ant-like by answering the question myself.

As a society in general, we've come a long way in regard to people with physical challenges. Thirty years ago there were no laws requiring handicapped accessibility like there is today. If you were disabled, you were restricted from entering a lot of public arenas. And think about it: Were there any TV programs depicting handicapped people interacting in "normal" situations? In spite of all the sex and violence on television today, in regard to disabilities, we now live in a kinder age. My heart waved yahoo flags when Heather Whitestone was crowned Miss America in 1995. Not because of her deafness, but because she faced her challenges and stunned the audience when she danced like a swan to Sandi Patti's "Via Dolorosa," which testified to her faith as well as her performance. She's one of my heroes.

One pet peeve I have is that most church pulpits are not handicap accessible. Only persons with physical limitations stager at the first glimpse of the height and steps of the pulpits in most of the newer sanctuaries. It seems that décor is considered over accessibility. Grandfather statutes may excuse older churches from making entrances and bathrooms handicap accessible, but I wish they would.

Prejudices are not limited to race and gender. With the exception of extremists, whites and blacks interact today with little thought to skin pigmentation; women really have come a long way; and finally, physically challenged people have a place in this world!

\* \* \*

Finding my place in the world as a physically challenged person has been like cooking pintos. First, I had to run my woe-is-me mindset through a sieve. That took time—years, actually. You see, I still had this picture of myself as incomplete if I couldn't sink a basket from mid court or walk with the swing of a budding teenager. My feminine ego wanted to turn heads because my physique moved with grace and charm, instead of people moving things so I could hobble by. When I entered a room, I wanted them to ask, "Which chair would you like?" as a courtesy to my femininity, rather than drawing attraction to my deformities. Mercy, I was plagued with fragments of residue that'd spoil any pot of beans!

All good southern cooks know that pintos need to cook slowly to get that thick, red soup that flavors them. And I did a lot of simmering as I snailed along. But every now and then, I'd lie down at night and it would dawn on me that I did something that day that I hadn't been able to do previously. It wasn't planned like the day I made two steps between the bars at therapy—it happened naturally, like a toddler who rattles off a complete sentence for the first time. It might not have been anything to wow about, but it was progress in the works just the same.

And when I got enough sense to season the little things with gratitude and a thankful heart, other delicacies came. I had the choice to view myself as a progressive miracle or expose myself, and everybody around me, to the scorched stench of self-pity. You cannot microwave negativism. It emanates through life lessons, listening to yourself and the criticism of others, and mostly, making a conscious effort to change. I was steeped in it from a childhood of listening to the words of adults who always pointed out the negatives. And frankly, it's hard sometimes to see the good when what you're feeling is bad. But for a child of God, there should always be something to be thankful for.

By reason of use, my dormant muscles gradually awoke. Steps were made and tasks performed because the desire to accomplish them was stronger than the pain the effort produced. Appreciation for family, friends, and life increased as my love and appreciation for my heavenly father and all he was doing in my life grew. How can we ask for more without daily acknowledgement and thankfulness for the everyday things we enjoy but so easily take for granted? The promise that mercy is new each morning got me through a heap of troubled nights.

Understand, my simmering period took years. When I came home from the center, I was thrust into the real world. Here people moved around me like a convoy of ants marching toward their individual Zions while I crept out of sync to the beat of a different drummer. During those initial years of adjustment and recovery, the black hole in my spirit mushroomed and I sank into a mental darkness that nobody but Jerry witnessed, and not even he could fathom its power.

I was like Pretty Boy darting precariously through a danger zone, up one minute and dashing into a window glassed with deception the next. Until I saw my cup as half full instead of half empty, I allowed my mind to stew on the past. I thought about the job I'd never return to; the soundless piano catching dust in our living room; my Toyota, destined to be sold; high-heels stacked in the closet waiting to go out of style; and the full-view mirror that I hated to look into.

That's about the time the two reoccurring dreams started. In one, I'm a senior in high school and discover that they've done away with girls' basketball. I go to Coach Jim Morgan in tears, begging him to do something—I have to play one more year. And then, there I am on the court in my lame-filled tennis shoes with a game in progress. I've got the ball, but I suddenly remember that I can no longer run. What am I going to do? Then calmness sweeps over me as I begin to dribble the ball. Everyone is expecting me to excel—they don't know that I can't run. So I start picking up speed. My feet are no longer touching the shiny gym floor. I'm gliding across the court now like a space rover. And I'm happy, so very happy!

In the other reoccurring dream I'm playing the piano. For a long time the song was "Amazing Grace," but then I started getting new songs. I can feel my fingers touching the keys with the fluidity of a ballerina. It seems so natural, as if I were an accomplished pianist. The words and melodies are virgin to my ears, but they're beautiful and soothing, always about Jesus. Then I remember that I can no longer use my fingers well enough to play the piano and the sound starts to grow faint. I beat the keys with fervor, but the piano dies—only the ears of my soul retain the music. I awake filled with peaceful harmony. But I cannot hold on to the tune that's bringing me peace. Even when I arise and scurry to capture it on paper, the intensity of the music slowly fades like a ship that meets the horizon—the best I can do is mingled with the natural. But until we can (literally) hear angels sing, what more can we mortals do?

\*   \*   \*

The enemy perched on my shoulder like a beastly leprechaun the night I sat up with a loaded pistol in my lap. I don't know why I did it. I guess sometimes you listen to him in a moment of weakness. I didn't understand the craziness in my head that was more paralyzing than the broken neck. From having been there, I think I can conclude that once an unnatural—certainly not God-given—thought pattern establishes itself, it sends out invitations for more life-suckers to join the party. Thank goodness, I had some of God's word in me, enough at least not to comply to the enemy's suggestions. But he got me to caress that pistol for a few hours. *Thy word have I his in mine heart, that I might not sin against thee* (Psalms 119:11). How important it is to fill our hearts with the word! Let the world call you a fanatic. The word in you will be the light that will guide your way when the darkness of the moment perpetuates a plummet.

I tried to make Jerry and Mama understand that something else was wrong with me besides the obvious external problems. But Jerry just looked at me, helpless for an answer. And Mama simply explained it away—after all, I'd been through a lot. So I made the mistake of pacifying the turmoil in my head by learning to avoid the things that seemed to irritate it.

The first big episode happened when I went back to the rehab center for therapy. I'd progressed from a walker to a three-pronged cane to a regular cane. Bonnie was walking me down the long hall that encircled the PT department, holding lightly to my arm. When she saw another patient who needed her attention, she let go of me and stepped away to help him. And then it happened: My toes curled inside my shoes like nubby claws and every muscle in my body coiled. If I'd had fingernails of any length, my left palm would have bled. My right hand became a vice around the cane handle. My blood rushed to my head, and I felt I'd surely disappear into the black and white speckled tile at any moment. Gravity was pulling my insides downward, and I wanted to yield, but a tornado couldn't have moved me— I was as stiff as a cold corpse and as hot as an iron. I burst into uncontrollable sobs. It was a ghastly scene! One that I didn't care to repeat.

Bonnie, shocked and forlorn, rushed back to me. "What's wrong, Sandra? What's wrong?"

I didn't know.

With my heart throbbing and strength drained, she led me to a mat and sat me down. When she saw that my problem didn't seem to be physical, she asked, "Do you think you need to talk with Dr. Faulkner?" he was the psychologist that I had spoken with briefly before discharge.

"No, I'll be okay," I told her. But I wasn't okay. I sunk deeper and deeper into the clutches of depression. The darkness within me distorted the good like vinegar added to wine, and ignorance held the mixture inside me like a corkscrew. If you'd asked my friends, parents, husband, or child if I was depressed, each would have said no. Depression was not a pliable consideration—that only happened to weirdos. Maybe it was because of my extreme circumstances—the trauma, the injury, the paralysis—that no one looked inward.

I somehow managed to wade through five years of uncertainty— my mind could not advance past twenty-four hours. If a day went by without an attack, I felt fortunate. Building our house helped take my mind off myself, but after we moved into our new home in 1977, the attacks seemed to escalate. I'd be ironing and suddenly wouldn't be able to turn loose of the iron. Or I'd start to take a cake from the oven and freeze. Mama took me on a lot of day trips, but if I'd loose sight of her in a department store, I'd start panicking. Venturing out on my own was unthinkable.

Valium seemed to be the only thing that would relax me. If I ran out, I'd call Grandpa Davis and he'd bring me some of his. My doctor prescribed them as a muscle relaxer, but I had to take them to keep calm at the grocery store, the doctor's office, and even at church. If our trio was scheduled to sing at a Sunday morning service, I would take a Valium so I could get to the front of the church and back without an incident. Thankfully, I did not become addicted.

When you're that depressed, tears are but a thought away. I think back at things that caused outbursts and wonder how I could have been so emotional. In desperation one day, I dropped to my knees in front of the window beside Kip's bed—where I often prayed—and cried out to God for help. I could no longer pretend to have it all together. I was free from the bonds of physical contraptions and I was institutionally free. But I'd never felt so entrapped.

# 15

## FOR LOVE'S SAKE

*We love him, because he first loved us.* —I John 4:19

T was December 1980 when I paid my first stomach-knotting visit to the psychiatrist in Winston-Salem. The way I found out about him was nothing short of a miracle. Yeah, I could have just looked in the yellow pages, or asked my family doctor, but I was waiting for God to lead me—I wasn't convinced that a "shrink" was the answer. Then a friend told me about her "nervous problems." As she elaborated, I realized her symptoms were similar to mine. What a coincidence! And this conversation took place shortly after my surrender and petition to God for help. She said she was advised to see a particular doctor, but didn't think she needed help at that point. I asked her for his number, because I did.

The doctor that my friend told me about wasn't taking any new patients, but I figured I didn't have anything to lose, so I said yes when the receptionist asked if I'd like to make an appointment with another psychiatrist. That first visit turned out to be quite revealing.

*       *       *

I mentally analyzed this psychiatrist: tweed trousers, pin-striped shirt, a skinny brown tie—nothing matched. He'd tried (without success) to flatten the curly strands of premature gray entwined among his uncontrollable head of once-blonde hair. I wanted to hypnotize him and free the ringlets he'd forced into his shirt collar. The pipe gave him an air of distinction as he reclined behind his mahogany desk. With that pink, flawless skin, he needed something to project that he was old enough for me to trust him with my sanity. Although he was clearly older than my thirty-one years, I still wished he were at least old enough to be my father. But does anyone fully trust a doctor or preacher who doesn't have crow's feet around the eyes and chicken scratching in his brow? You know, marks of the trade.

I wondered what he was thinking about me. Did he see me or the ugly black cane and limp? At least the obvious affliction was proof that I had a problem, but the plague that warranted this visit was invisible. The limp, he couldn't help, but the emotional scars, I prayed he could.

Sunk down in the soft leather of his ebony chair, he took a puff off his pipe, picked up his ballpoint pen, and then brought his eyes to mine. "What seems to be the problem?"

I briefed him on the accident, and then said, "I'm a quadriplegic."

"No, you might have been a quadriplegic," he corrected me, with a shy smile. "Quadriplegics don't walk."

"Well, I mean…I was…uh, the Lord touched me," I stammered, feeling stupid for not being able to express myself, and the comment I blurted out about the Lord seemed scant. "Anyway, the reason I'm here is…" and I began to explain the specifics of the "attacks to my brain."

This is where the good doctor started to probe: Did I have a good marital relationship? Did I have a good childhood? Was I popular in school?

I started to squirm. *Maybe coming here was a mistake,* I thought. But I was there, so I answered his questions—vaguely. And then he lowered the boom: "What do you do for fun?"

*You educated, baby-faced, pipe-puffing fool! Can't you see that I've lost the ability to have "fun"?* my mind responded. He scribbled on his clipboard, letting the silence between us fill him in. As I searched for an answer, a picture flashed through my mind: I'm running from my car in the parking lot at Western Electric, taking the steps by twos as I passed the guard in an effort to beat the clock. In our yard at the trailer and through the path in the woods to Grandma's. From our neighbor's angry dog. On the basketball court. At play with my child.

*Why am I associating fun with running? He means now, what do I do for fun now?*

Still, no answer. I thought of my fingers flying across my keypunch machine, joining efforts with my colleagues to get the payroll finished by quitting time every Tuesday night. I saw my hands filling out my weekly time card: employee number 54216, department number 12WL316512. I hadn't associated my job with *fun* before.

I thought about the two songs that had just "come to me," and the joy I derived from playing them on the piano and singing them at church. How my spirit had connected with my mind to blend the words with music. And how that could never happen again. And I thought of the ditched dream of one day becoming proficient on the piano, or at least better, now that I really wanted to.

I sighed.

The doctor didn't seem to be in a particular hurry—he must have asked that question before and heard the same response. So I followed my thoughts.

I saw myself climbing into a treestand with Jerry in the mountains where he loved to hunt, and almost shivered at the thought of his icy hands inside my shirt in his attempt to warm them. I filed that one for later recall.

I relived the feeling of control that revving the gas and changing the gears on our long-gone-but-dear-to-heart Firebird had ignited the day I was clocked going sixty-four in a forty-five mph zone. I thought about how I charmed the patrolman out of writing me a ticket. The recollection almost made me smile.

I thought of the last time I rode a horse, the wind blowing in my face and the exhilaration of the cantering animal beneath me. I felt like pitching a this-ain't-fair fit!

I had no alternative but to deal with the psychiatrist's question: "What do you do for fun?" I was clueless as to anything I did now—just for me—for the pure pleasure of it. I couldn't even think of a lie.

Of course, I found joy in my son. And I could think of lots of things that he and Jerry did for fun, and I enjoyed watching them. But I was pretty sure that didn't count. What did my not having fun have to do with these attacks, anyway?

Obviously, a lot.

I wanted the man on the other side of the mahogany desk to give me a simple, smoker's-voice solution, such as: You have a chemical imbalance, post-trauma syndrome, caused by an injury to the central nervous system. Here's a pill. Take it, and the devil will leave you alone.

But is anything that simple? He did prescribe a pill, and thank God it helped the imbalance, post-trauma syndrome, depression, hell-sent whatever. But looking back on years of trying to balance through a seesaw of emotions—up one minute, down the next—I found a simple truth that's worth more than all the therapy and mind-probing one could attain. Are you ready? *A merry heart doeth good like a medicine, but a broken spirit drieth the bones* (Proverbs 17:22).

No one is happy all the time, but everyone should have something they do simply because they enjoy it. Fun doesn't have to be participating in a sport, although if I could, I would. I wouldn't be afraid to bet my eyetooth on my personal theory that God created the human spirit to be productive and actively participating in some type of creativity. Fun means something different to everyone, and it changes with the seasons of our lives. It may be roping a calf at the rodeo at twenty and playing bingo at eighty-five, but by George you'd better find time for whatever it is that leaves you with a sense of fulfillment or as sure as a rainless summer scorches the earth, you'll dry up!

I was drying up inside, because fun was connected to activity my body would no longer allow. Could my performer's spirit actually have been a God-given vent? I believe so. The need to create, perform, and even compete still rushed through me like a torrent. My inner self was screaming for a place to participate in a passion. I've never been one who sits gracefully on the sidelines. I felt violated by the turn my life had taken. It wasn't supposed to be this way. I felt blessed to be doing what I wasn't supposed to be able to do: walk. But I was as void as a candle with no flame. I could not peer past the doctor's pipe and pose and years of study and say with confidence, "Hey, doc, you're on the wrong track." He'd hit a nerve, and it stung like a sniper's bullet. It was a just-the-facts-Ma'am question, and I was as transparent as a drinking glass—and just as empty.

But here's the good part: Jesus is waiting for us to strip off the faux humility—he sees right through us, anyway. He compelled me to rest on him, the creator of creativity. So I crawled atop the Rock of Ages and pulled my knees under my chin, as the winds of insecurity beat against my hollow sanctuary. Well…actually, I was leaning against the side of our house, waiting for Mama to come and rescue me from my can't-help-it situation and take me somewhere, anywhere to get my mind off my troubles for a little while.

That's when I looked through teary eyes into a marshmallow sky and cried, "Please, make it better." I wasn't asking for healing, necessarily, although I didn't dismiss the possibility. It was more of a plea for a sense of belonging, a way to contribute what I had left in turn for fulfillment—a life, not spent, but lived.

And like that slow-moving train on a drizzling day, the answer came. There was music left in me that a fractured body could not suppress, and each time it surfaced, I was stimulated. I didn't say it was good, I said I was stimulated. That's what creativity allowed to surface does: stimulates, invigorates, and oils dry bones. It started so simplistically that I didn't even know anything was starting. Notes taken during Sunday morning sermons, strums on an omnicord, little bites of scripture put to music. Taking time to observe God's handiwork—he's designed enough of himself in nature to inspire masterpieces. And learning to quiet my mind, so I could hear my spirit.

I didn't understand that unleashing passion was the answer. When it had tried before to surface, I'd stifled it with a "Yeah, but I've got this disability thing." But music was bubbling in my spirit. Maybe not the kind that would produce a masterpiece, but passions don't necessarily have to shine to those around you. Simple songs satisfied me. Even a mere bubble of a passion needs a place to vent. It's unhealthy to suppress Godly passions. And if he plants a seed within you, you will have a passion to nurture it to harvest.

I don't mean to be so hard on myself; revelation doesn't always come instantaneously, and a loss like I sustained takes time to get used to, thank you very much. But if I've learned anything out of the process, I've learned that self pity stifles passions. And I've done enough hard time in the dungeon of its seclusion. Cindi Allen's comment to me one day has risen to haunt me on several occasions. "What do I have left?" I asked her.

"Your mind!" she replied.

And then finally one day it hit me: Fingers don't write songs! It wouldn't matter if I had a hundred good fingers, without my mind (soul and emotions) I could never write a song. God did not take the gift and ear for music away because my fingers curl from spasticity. I had written nine-and-a-half songs, and they wouldn't leave me alone. I ran across a magazine ad about a recording studio in Mt. Airy, and on a whim I called. I explained that I had written some songs and wondered what it would cost to do a demo to send to "real" gospel singers. Of course, they wanted me to come the next day to discuss it.

I didn't have an inkling of knowledge about the recording industry. But those songs kept twirling, twirling...so, whom do I call? Mama. And she and I drove to Mt. Airy the next day like two blonde...mice?

"Twelve hundred dollars?" I echoed when the man gave me a price. "But I don't need two hundred tapes!"

\* \* \*

My hands were shaking the day my two hundred cassettes arrived in the mail. I held one in my hand and was jolted by my picture on the front cover, as if I were actually somebody who should do such thing. I unwrapped the cellophane and stuck the tape in my jam box, but before I pushed "play," I prayed, *Lord, please touch people's ears and make this sound good to them, or I'm stuck with two hundred tapes that I don't know what to do with!* Not to mention, I had borrowed money from my dad to get them shipped to me from the tape manufacturer, due to a bad working relationship they had with the recording studio that I had (blindly) trusted.

As the first song and title of my recording began to play, I wept, remembering where I was when the words came, and where the Lord had brought me from.

—— *For Love's Sake* ——

*The great Shepherd of the sheep watches over me*
*Though I stray from his side he reaches tenderly*
*Draws me back into his fold and securely he holds*
*Day by day, along the way*
*For love's sake*
*I was dead in sin when he quickened me*
*Raised me up to new heights so the Son I could see*
*And his love knows no end; on him I depend*
*He gave his all to save my soul*
*For love's sake*
*For love's sake he lifted me*
*From bonds of sin and set me free*
*For love's sake through eternity*
*I'll live again*
*For love's sake*

When my former English teacher Norm Barnes called and asked if I would come to East Bend Friends Meeting (where he was pastor) on a particular Sunday morning and "hold a concert," I laughed. "I've never done a concert," I told him.

"Well, can you still come and sing the songs that are on this tape?"

"I don't have anybody to accompany me," I said. But he insisted I try to work something out. I hung up dazzled.

A few days later I received a call from someone at Prospect United Methodist Church wanting me to do the same thing—a concert—on that same Sunday, but in the evening instead. I was getting a suspicion that God was up to something.

I told Jerry about the invitations and that I needed to find somebody to accompany me on piano so I could perform at both churches. His reply was: "I don't want anything to do with it!" And he lived up to his proclamation. I met with a few people who might be able to play my songs by just listening to them, but nothing worked out. Then I got to thinking that maybe the studio where I recorded could take my voice out to make sound tracks. I hesitated to deal with them again after a bad experience in acquiring my tapes, but I didn't know what else to do. The musicians I'd worked with had been great, so I took a chance, and gave the studio a call.

I'd already secured a loan for the initial amount I had to pay on the day I did the recording, so I called Becky Hobson, friend and "personal banker," and asked if she'd give me a loan for a sound system without Jerry's signature. "Of course," she said. That was all I needed to hear. I drove (a big deal in itself) to Winston-Salem and bought a small sound system. When I returned home, I asked Jerry if he would mind unloading it. I believe he was more scared than shocked at my tenacity. The guy that I bought the sound system from wanted me to do nightclubs with him. "We can make a couple of hundred a night," he said. The money sounded good, but I hadn't heard "nightclub" in God's direction. I really needed to know I had a way to repay my daddy for the loan he gave me, but I would trust God.

Jerry went with me to those first two churches, and many more to come, but sometimes, in those early years, I never knew until the last minute if he'd go or balk. It was becoming clearer to me that God was moving me into a singing ministry, but Jerry never felt the calling. He went along because I needed him, but there was a wedge between us that my passion to sing only seemed to widen. I don't know if he felt intimated by the way singing energized me, or if he simply hated having a second job, which is understandable, but his lack of enthusiasm dumped water on my fire on many occasions. And I felt guilty for imposing my passion on him just because I couldn't do it alone.

And wouldn't this vulnerable time in our lives be another easy kill for the enemy? Oh yes, and the devil jumped in with both feet. He not only wanted to destroy our marriage and home, but he wanted to pluck up any good seeds my songs and story of healing had planted. I can't blame my bad decisions on the devil, as if I didn't have a say in them, nor can Jerry. But the enemy attacked at our weakest link and left us sinking in a sea of regret.

The story of our transgressions and love triangles would make a good movie, but I don't feel as if I should glorify our misgivings with details. It seems like my whole life has been filled with disillusions. Somewhere along the way I conditioned myself not to get too excited when something worthwhile came along, because it could leave just as quickly. But the best of times has always been when I was in the middle of something I'm passionate about. Religion tried to sell me the lie that once you fail you can never be useful to God again. And I almost bought it. But even in the down times, writing songs kept me from going under. I didn't always have an audience, but I knew that eventually I would because the creative juices were flowing.

By 1990 I had fallen down, got up, and brushed myself off so many times that dips and peaks in my spirit were almost the norm. But God was proving himself strong and moving in unusual ways to bless me. Jerry's interest in the ministry was growing, and I had been praying for money to come in to do a fourth recording project. I also needed guidance as to the right place to record. I'd made enough mistakes, and I was tired of borrowing money from my parents and the bank. But the day that I received a telephone call from a man named Woody Peoples, I was overwhelmed with the goodness of God.

"Do you remember me?" Woody asked. He explained that he was the choir director at a church I had been to a few times. I immediately recalled him as being a tall, very kind man, probably in his seventies, who had signed my mailing list. He preceded to tell me about his wife Callie who had recently passed away. They had no children, and his loneliness since her passing had almost consumed him. "God told me the last time you were at our church to put you in my will," he said. "I want you to do that recording you're wanting to do."

Emotion flooded me. Why would a near stranger do such a thing? The only reason was a good heart and God told him to do it. "Woody, that's so sweet of you," I told him, "but I might go before you."

"Well, I've already gone to my lawyer and had you included," he said. "I wasn't going to tell you, but then I got to thinking, what would your husband think if you got a call that you were in some man's will? I didn't want to cause any trouble with your husband."

After that, Woody visited every place he could where I was singing, and Jerry and I got a chance to get to know him. Two months later Woody discovered he had cancer. He lived only a few weeks and then joined Callie in heaven. There were fourteen people, as I recall, in his will. I think he would have rescued every needy soul in the world if he could have. Woody worked hard his entire life and never lived above his means—I know he's rich now beyond measure. From his obedience, we were able to buy a used van to travel in and pay cash for my "Keepsake" project, which is dedicated to the memory of Woodrow Wilson Peoples.

I ended up signing a contract with Heartlook Records, a division of the Mark V Record Company, in exchange for publishing rights to all the songs. My producer chose "Forever in His Arms" as the first radio single, and I decided to hire a radio promoter for as long as I could afford it. Surprisingly, the song hit the top eighty list and continued to climb in the *Singing News* charts. It debuted in *Gospel Voice* magazine at number thirty-four. We turned around and sent out the second single, "There'll Be Peace in the Valley (When He Comes)," when the first song fell off the charts. I was humbled (and ecstatic) when it made the gospel charts as well. I also found country gospel music to be big in the Netherlands. Several songs from "Keepsake" charted in the top ten there, including these two released in the states. *The Country Gazette*, a secular country music magazine in the Netherlands, did an article on me in Dutch. I was listed among the *Who's Who in the Gospel Voice* in 1994 because I had produced a top forty song. Local bookings were steadily coming in as my voice was heard over the airwaves.

After my first radio release hit the charts, my radio promoter called to tell me the Christian Country Music Association had nominated me for the "Female Vocalist" category. It was requested that I perform on stage at their inaugural awards benefit in Nashville, Tennessee. I was dazed. I had not even anticipated a singing ministry when I did that first little experiment in 1984. Now, almost ten years and a thousand obstacles later, my songs were being played in places I'd never heard of. And I didn't think I was "able" physically or emotionally to follow through with any of it. I was diagnosed with agoraphobia (the fear of open spaces), likely to have a major panic attack at any time, and I was told I'd be performing on stage in Nashville.

While all this was going on in my life, Jerry was struggling with his own problems. He moved out of our home just before my trip to the CCMA awards. I begged Jerry to go with me, but he couldn't. A bus tour was organized and family members and friends signed up to go along and support me. But despite the encouragement surrounding me, I couldn't have felt more alone had I hitchhiked all the way.

Right before I entered the stage on the night of my performance, a Plexiglas podium was positioned as a prop for me, and a handsome cowboy with a ten-gallon hat escorted me onto the stage. But as soon as he walked away and I was forced to look into the glaring lights, I felt my toes curling under in my fancy, white boots. But live or die, I was determined not to let my panic be known. Each group or soloist was allowed three songs. I began with "There'll Be Peace in the Valley," the peppy tune I'd written with a lot of soul.

The intense lighting prevented me from seeing the audience. I'm accustomed to looking at people when I sing, and I needed that connection with my audience. But I couldn't see past the glare. The crowd clapped at the end of my first song, but I couldn't tell why. You learn to read people after ten years of singing to crowds. I wanted to stop the show and shout, "Hey, lower the lights so I can see some eyeballs!" And if I'd been in a church, that's exactly what I'd have done.

By the time the second track started for "Forever in His Arms," I had loosening up a tad. For the last number, I sang a rewritten version of "Unchained Melody" instead of a song I'd written. I don't know what possessed me considering all the tunes I could of picked, except perhaps my melancholy state with Jerry gone. I rewrote it as a prayer: *Oh, my Lord, my Father, I've hungered for your touch…*

All of my sweet friends raved about how good it was, and I was even invited to perform Sunday morning at a local church while in Nashville. Unfortunately, I had to decline as the bus was scheduled to leave for home early Sunday. When we loaded the bus after my performance to head back to the motel, Mama jumped me, "Why in the world did you sing that song? Why didn't you sing 'Imagine'? The first two were good, but you should have sung 'Imagine' [her favorite]!"

I've hated "Unchained Melody" ever since.

I basically went through the motions that weekend in August of 1993, knowing it was an experience to remember. I wasn't assigned a roommate, just in case Jerry changed his mind. Everyone kept asking if I was sure I wanted to stay by myself? Actually, no, I didn't. When I took my showers before getting ready to go to the singing each of the three nights, I literally had to fall out of the tub to get out. But I was determined to do what I had to do. I hated myself for needing Jerry so much, for needing help from anybody for that matter. And I've never wished I could hate a man like I wanted to hate him. But my love for him refused to die. "It'll take some time, but you'll get used to being without him," friends told me.

The woman that traveled along to do my makeup and hair spent the last night with me in my room, and it was good to have an ear to bend until sleep overtook us. I think if I'd stayed much longer in the emotional state I was in, my bones would have dried up for sure. My skin was flaking to the point that I had to constantly apply moisturizers. I kept hard candy or cough drops in my mouth every waking minute to prevent my lips from sticking to my teeth. My body had become a dry well.

I was never so glad to see Carolina soil after that three-day excursion. But I came home to quit singing altogether. I had no passion left but to restore the marriage that everyone but Kip (and me on a good day) seemed sure had died. I could elaborate on how our son's prayers have kept our heads above water during several stormy spans, but he wouldn't want me to, and I'll respect that. But Jerry and I will both confess that Kip has been the wind that's kept us assail. Jerry came back home—of his own free will and to the surprise of many—after three months. Small towns are notorious for gossip, and East Bend is no exception. We were supposed to be "spiritual examples," but we're humans, and humans have problems and make mistakes.

I suppose the hardest thing for me has been feeling as though I'm inflicting Jerry with my disability. He's stuck through many hardships, and who would've blamed him if he'd bailed out for good? For a long time I believed that every negative thing that happened between us was because of the way I am. He says that's ridiculous, but it's hard for me to think otherwise. When we leaped into marriage, I had no ambition or passion to be anything but a wife and mother. I don't think

Jerry thought about it either way; he just lived for the moment. How short-sighted of both of us! I thought his love would be the only salve I'd ever need to solve any problem. But I found that hinging my happiness on his love for me was like pinning a barrel on his lapel for him to carry each day. We're opposites in outlook and desires, and that's something neither can change. We've certainly worked through more "stuff" than most couples would be willing to in this day and age.

As for the music ministry, we traveled sparsely during the rest of the nineties, but that passion never really returned. Looking back, I don't think either of us had the stability to withstand the pitfalls in the early years. I know the Lord used us, and whether Jerry ever recognized it or not, his support of me was an inspiration to many. But after we resolved our problems, my focus for ministry changed. I charged into services like a bull with an attitude. I was burned out with telling my "big toe story." I wanted to save the world! I started doing more sharing, much to the regret of many who thought I was preaching. But I sought God before meetings, and if he spoke something to me, I felt obligated to share it. At the end of my singing/sharing, I started offering people an opportunity to come forward so I could pray for their needs. And they came, too, many of them, often loaded with a heavy burden. Some, I'm glad to say, received Christ. But much to my dismay, there were ministers who didn't like the idea of a woman speaking the word from their pulpits. And I think a few had a problem with their people responding. I found out that some ministers had even black labeled me. "Don't invite her," they'd tell their pastor friends. Some called me "the singing preacher." And yes, it hurt. But I must add that the majority of churches and pastors have received what I have to offer with gratitude. What else can I be but what I am?

I still love to sing, and I'm appreciative of the churches that allow me a voice. But I've found that passions change—the need to be passionate about something doesn't. My family and taking my writing to a new and different level are now my heartthrobs. And I believe that if I lose the passion to write, something else will emerge from inside me. I've stopped letting circumstances, people, and my own self-motivated humility thwart the gift of creativity God put in me before I emerged from the womb. To have no passion is suicide, and I'm not ready to succumb. I may not be able to run or use my hands for some things like I used to, but ask me what I do for fun, and I won't grope for an answer. God's love will see to that!

# AFTERWORD

*Thou hast turned for me my mourning into dancing: thou hast put off my sackcloth and girded me with gladness; to the end that my glory may sing praise to thee, and not be silent. O Lord my God, I will give thanks unto thee forever.* —Psalms 30:11–12

THINGS HAVE CERTAINLY changed at our house since my accident in 1975. I feel as though I've been two different people wrapped up in one life: a typical country girl turned woman without much vision for the future, and a woman with a lot of little girl left to tame before facing a mountain of challenges.

When I was small I prayed that I would die before my parents, so I wouldn't have to face the agony of losing them. My prayer since the accident has been that my parents would live to see me totally healed. And I know I can't turn back the clock, but I dream of giving back to Jerry the wife of his youth. If I never get to climb into a deerstand with him again, though, we will always have our special moments.

Like all children, Kip and Mark grew up—several years ago. I hope they recall the times I took them swimming at Tanglewood Park and played Frisbee in the yard, but those memories are more vivid to me, I'm sure. The important thing is that they glean from the lessons life has dealt them, and I pray that my challenges have inspired them to live life to its fullest and love like there's no tomorrow.

Kip married April Choplin on October 3, 1999. I don't think it was an accident that they (unknowingly) chose the date of the anniversary of my accident to marry; I now have a happy memory for that day.

Mark's marriage to Melissa Pilcher in 1995 brought him a wife and a four-year-old stepson, Matthew Ryan. God's timing is always right—

*(back row): Jake, Kip, Jerry; (middle row): Sandra, Melissa, Mark, Ruth, Matthew; (in floor): April, Noah, and Morgan.*

Matthew's presence healed a lot of hurts in our family. The first time I saw him in my mother's arms, I knew this shy little dark-haired boy was meant to be a part of our lives. Morgan Tyler joined us February 21, 1997 to complete Mark's family. Morgan is a chocolate-eyed repeat of his dad and a treat to us all.

Noah Jake was born to Kip and April on May 3, 2001. His blonde hair is not as platinum as Kip's when he was small, but in most every other way he is Kip all over again. You can imagine what that does for Jerry and me. I look at Morgan and Noah together and have to bite my tongue to keep from calling them by their daddy's names. What a special gift God reserves for us as we age! And by the time this book is out, we should be grandparents for the second time. I can't wait!

I'm glad I persevered through the hard times and mountain moving. My calamity at age twenty-six not only meant an adjustment for me, but the rest of my family as well, especially Jerry. Indeed, no man (or woman) is an island—what affects you, affects those closest to you. We neither live nor die to ourselves. And as I embark toward new adventures, I'm thankful that God will already be there when I arrive. I'll look back occasionally and draw strength from the mountains I was fortunate enough to watch him move.

*I thought about the former days, the years of long ago; and I remembered my songs in the night. My heart mused and my spirit inquired: Will the Lord reject me forever? Will he show his mercy again? Has his unfailing love vanished forever? Has his promise failed for all time? Has God forgotten to be merciful? Has he in anger withheld his compassion? Then I thought, "To this I will appeal: the years of the right hand of the Most High." I will remember the deeds of the Lord; yes, I will remember your miracles of long ago* (Psalms 77:5–11 NIV).

Writing this memoir has allowed a reconnection with my past—good times and bad—and has served to bring closure to pain I needed to vent. The writing process (soul searching, digging, and burying old wounds) has been healing. I've never felt as close to God as when I'm writing. I think writing is what I'm here to do during this season of life. God says I'm a performer, and he loves me just as I am. So with that in mind:

*I'll sing and I'll write*
*I'll be Mama, Grammy, and wife*
*Until I fly away…*

Blessings,

*Sandra*

# ACKNOWLEDGMENTS

I MUST FIRST THANK MY Lord and Savior Jesus Christ for instilling in me the passion to write this book. The Holy Spirit has truly been my teacher and guide throughout the years of preparation, given me the inspiration to pen my thoughts, and finally the release to make it happen.

Thank you Jerry for allowing me to share our personal lives. You have graciously given me the space to be creative and loved me through the process. My triumphs and valleys have been yours, and your valor runs like a thread through every page.

Thank you Kip, April, and Noah for squeezing out of me more love than I knew I had. I pray this book will be a keepsake for you to pass along to those you love.

Thank you Mama for all the running and fixing and for holding your breath while I revealed your fun-loving personality and stubborn grit to the world.

Thank you Daddy for giving me a solid-rock foundation from the beginning. Without it, my story could have taken a different turn.

Thank you Mark, Melissa, Matthew, and Morgan for your moral support and love. Mark, your hand has been a tangible strength many times when storms have been too rough for me to stand. Thanks, too, Melissa for sharing your gift of photography.

Thank you Troy and Gladys Miller for being the best in-laws anyone could have. And thanks for making Jerry!

Thank you Ann, Linda, Jeanette and families for your prayers and for accepting me as I am.

Thank you Melissa James for devoting yourself to keeping my body in tune with your healing hands.

Thank you Scott Whitaker for your patience and labor in making this book design the best for God's glory.

Thanks a million, Emily-Sarah Lineback, for being the best editor God could have sent. You have enriched my life.

# ABOUT THE AUTHOR

SANDRA MILLER IS A book editor for regional publisher Carolina Avenue Press, and her writings appear in several publications including *Yadkin Valley Living* magazine, where she is a regular bimonthly columnist.

Miller is also a songwriter and singer, with songs that have hit the charts in the United States and overseas. In 1993 she was nominated for "Female Vocalist" by the Christian Country Music Association. She has performed on various stages and has appeared on "The 700 Club." Miller continues to perform as a guest singer and inspirational speaker for numerous groups and organizations.

Miller lives with her husband, Jerry, in East Bend, North Carolina, where she enjoys spending time with her family, painting, reading, and playing outdoors on a four-wheeler. *When Mountains Move* is her first book.

# AUTHOR'S NOTE

IF YOU HAVE ANY QUESTIONS or comments about this book, want to order additional copies, need to inquire about bulk discount rates, or would like to set up an inspirational speaking/singing event with Sandra Miller, please contact:

**Lovesake**
PUBLISHING

4324 Mount Bethel Church Road
East Bend, North Carolina 27018
www.sandramillerministries.com
*e-mail:* lovesake@msn.com

# PRAISE FOR THE
# AUTHOR'S SONGWRITING

" Sandra Miller is a wonderful songwriter. Her lyrics are true to the Word of God, with melodies that will lift the listener's spirits. I believe we'll be hearing a lot of her tunes on radio for years to come."

TINA SADLER,
*Two-time Dove Winner*

" Sandra Miller is a writer that is certainly used by God to pen fresh and anointed songs. She reaches into the depths of her heart and God's word for her music.

SHAREN ALEXANDER,
*Rose of Sharen Productions*

" Sandra Miller is committed and it shows, committed to the cause of Christ. I appreciate her dedication to our blessed Lord, and for her giving her talents to God."

LARRY PETREE,
*Award-winning songwriter*